INTERPRETING YOUR DREAMS

Nature's Path to Self-Knowledge

By

W. Lindsay Jacob, M.D.

Copyright © 1984 W. Lindsay Jacob, M.D.
All Rights Reserved

Published By

J.POHL ASSOCIATES
461 Spring Run Road
Coraopolis, PA 15108

ISBN 0-939332-06-X

Cover Design by T. W. McKenzie

Dedicated To
Kathie, My Wife,
And To
Everett Irion,
The Other Person
I Tell My Dreams To

ACKNOWLEDGMENTS

To TAYE SIMONDS TOWNLEY, whose literary expertise was of great help in preparing some of the original drafts of this manuscript. Many of her well-turned phrases still appear throughout the book.

To SHIRLEY HAVILAND, who first managed to create this book from my lecture tapes and then became involved once again in its final preparation.

CHAPTER I

Why Do We Dream?

The human condition is truly remarkable. We all go through our round of days experiencing more or less the same kinds of things. Yet each of us makes our own separate reality of our life experience on this planet Earth. We do this to such an extent that it seems the only real working definition of truth we have is: what is true for an individual is what he can take and grow on. It certainly does appear that "what is one man's meat is another man's poison."

Underlying this separateness, however, there is a unity. We all have the same bodies despite our coloring. We all must eat and sleep and devise protection against the elements. And when we sleep, we all dream. We lie down to sleep at night, toss and turn a bit and wake up the next morning saying, "I had the craziest dream last night." Sometimes the dream sticks with us for awhile the next day. We muse about it on the way to work or think about it in the occasional off-moments we have during the morning. Usually it fades out during the day to be forgotten with most of the rest of our dreams.

Occasionally a dream cannot be ignored. It makes an impression on us that may last for years and years. It is then that some of us come to realize there must be something more to this process of dreaming than the silly, sometimes frightening, sometimes pleasant occurrences of our sleep. Most people are naturally intrigued by their dreams and try to obtain information or guidance from them. Some do this in an organized way and some rather casually. When you talk to groups of people about dreams, however, there is an immediate response. They seem to be instinctively aware that there is a tremendous amount of information in our dreams if we can only decipher it. This immediate response, with some adequate instruction, can easily be turned into a more than passing interest. Over the years I have been able to teach people the simple basics of working with their own dreams, thereby giving them a method of self-help that will be useful for the rest of their lives.

True enough, there are some people who really don't care about their dreams and seldom recall them the next day. But with most people, the response to information contained in their dreams is so marked and so enthusiastic that there seems to be no question in their minds that there really is something there worth knowing. The question, of course, is: "What is it, and how do you get at it?" The rest of this book will be devoted to these specific details. In Chapter I, I think it important to give an overall view of the subject and try to answer that basic question, "What is dreaming and what is its purpose?"

Where Do Dreams Come From?

As we have already indicated, dreaming is something that everybody does. Furthermore, it is something that everybody does while they are asleep and seemingly have no control over it. Nightmares come whether we are afraid of them or not, and pleasant dreams often occur when we least expect them. When we wake up and review the dream we have had, it seems to have been an entirely spontaneous production, when, in reality, it was skillfully created by our subconscious mind.

Dreams often seem so spontaneous that the ancients took them as messages from the gods or from the individual's soul. Maybe they weren't so far wrong. I firmly believe that we each have a soul—not some vague pink cloud that follows us around but an integral part of our personality—whether we realize it or not. It is possible that, while we are sleeping, the dream is really our soul talking to us in its own particular way. If this is so, it may be why Jesus did much of his teaching in parables. He was trying to reach men's souls and perhaps felt that using the soul's way of communicating in consciousness, instead of in the dream state, might be more effective.

On the other hand, there seems to be building up a body of evidence that dreams are produced by the computer which we call the brain. It clears its banks each evening, filing and refiling the data received during the day, and in the process stirs up emotional responses and reactions that arise in the form of dreams. There is no question that a certain amount of validity must be attributed to this theory as well.

I feel that both theories play a part in the genesis of our dreams. Nature is quite miraculous for its economy of functioning and there is no reason why both of these processes could not have their input into an individual's dream.

The Subconscious According To Freud

There is also the phenomenon of the subconscious mind. Sigmund Freud started modern man's reawakened interest in dreams by publishing his famous book on the subject in 1900. He attributed dreams to the functioning of the subconscious mind, which he called the "id," and described them as being primitive, pleasure seeking and very much sexually oriented. He felt that the drives and instincts of the subconscious mind met with the ego, the consciousness, in sleep, and the result was dreams and dreaming. In the process of doing so, Freud rather badly confused our more fundamental drives and instincts with nonverbal thinking. As a result, his writings show dreams as the expression of infantile wishes, largely sexual in nature, that have to be censored or hidden from our conscious awareness.

Then Freud went on to talk about the type of thinking that is involved in the production of dreams and its many subtle and complicated patterns of association. In his attempt to delineate these processes and to be strictly scientific, Freud completely ignored the possibility that the individual's soul might be involved in the dreaming process as well. The closest he came to the idea of soul was his concept of "super ego," which he felt was a sort of conscience inculcated into us by the rules and regulations of our family and society.

Biblical Dreams And Visions

The ancients didn't know about the super ego. But, whether they were in the East or in the West, they were very much concerned about their souls. And when they had dreams, they tended to pay attention to them. They believed that the soul, or perhaps the gods, were attempting to give them a message of some kind. It is because of this attitude about dreaming that the Christian Church exists as it is today. Matthew records that the Holy Family fled into Egypt and returned on the advice of their dreams. It was also their dreams that led them to settle in Nazareth. Thus it was that the life of Jesus was saved and his education and training, or at least his early experiences, were influenced by the types of dreams his parents were having.

There is also that interesting series of visions (that may not have been dreams) recorded in the Acts of the Apostles. They were experienced by Peter and a man named Cornelius and resulted in Peter deciding to accept the Gentiles, as well as his Jewish brethren, into his beginning church. Had this not happened, Christianity might only be a small sub-sect of Judaism today.

There are literally hundreds of examples of dreams and their results in the Bible. These are merely a few that have had a very direct effect upon the history of the world and the Christian majority that exists in the West. Incidentally, similar stories can be told for the development of Islam. They exist in the histories of the Far East as well.

The Fundamental Nature Of The Dreaming Process

As this book goes on, you will hear much more about the ancient lore of dreams—and an occasional story of how dreams have influenced individuals who, in turn, influenced history. But at this point, it is important that we begin to understand the fundamental nature of the dreaming process. The dictionary defines dreaming as any sensory experience that occurs while we are asleep. This is quite correct in that dreams can and do utilize all of the sensory modalities in their production. Most often it is the senses of sight, sound and feeling that are present—but touch and smell can also occur from time to time. This definition seems somehow inadequate in that it does not address the purpose of dreaming. Why is it that, after we fall asleep, we experience these dreams that can be so ridiculous, sublime, terrifying or pleasant —and which often seem to haunt us with some sort of hidden meaning? The fundamentals of the biological mechanics of dreams and dreaming are outlined in Chapter IV. However, these careful scientific studies and measurements don't seem to give much clue as to the individual purpose behind this very human phenomenon.

I call dreams a human phenomenon even though it is perfectly obvious to any of us who own a dog or a cat that animals dream as well. Human beings seem to be the only creatures on Earth that are confounded or concerned about the nature of their dreams and dreaming. Being human and being aware of being aware seems to make the difference between the dreams of animals and ourselves. It is the one factor that thus far we have been unable to measure in the sleep laboratories around the world. We share a great deal with the animals, including the process of dreaming, but, as humans, we are somehow capable of making more of it than the animals are able to do. When we lie down to sleep there is a greater depth and meaning to the dream process than there seems to be for our animal friends. Whether this increased depth comes from our greater intelligence and self-awareness, or whether it comes from having a soul, is a question that the individual dreamer will have to answer for himself.

The Purpose Of Dreaming

The purpose of dreaming is to interpret the nature of the reality we are making for ourselves. As we go through life we all experience similar things—but each of our experiences is unique and individual depending upon our background, our viewpoints and how we placed ourselves in the situation we experienced. Nonetheless, the actual awareness of every moment of our lives comes to us primarily through our senses, which give us information both about the world outside and the world inside of ourselves. In other words, our senses tell us what is happening to us and what we are trying to do in any given situation. Once we have gained this fundamental information, we immediately start to think about it in abstractions or thought forms which we call words. By doing so, we add a whole new dimension to our experience of whatever the situation happens to be. We get so good at thinking in these abstractions we call words that we tend to lose track of the more fundamental nature of our awarenesses. We become so overbalanced in this way of thinking that most of our behaviors are the result of abstractions (words) that are far removed from our being.

Let me give you an example of what I am talking about here. The scene is at a swimming pool where a father and his three-year-old son are enjoying the water. The three-year-old feels like he has to urinate and simply lowers his trunks and urinates with considerable aplomb into the swimming pool. The father laughs, but then tries to explain to the youngster why his behavior is not appropriate. When he, the father, has to urinate, he goes to the toilet by the showers. The three-year-old hasn't learned that many words yet, and the emotions that go with them, so his solution to his awareness of his need is simple and direct. The father has learned a lot of words about a lot of social behaviors, so his solution is more circumspect. The difference in their behavior is due to the fact that the youngster has not learned enough words yet to understand the nuances of proper social conduct.

Oddly enough, when the youngster grows up, he cannot recall the event—as is the case with most of his life prior to the age of five or so. This is due to the fact that he now thinks so much in words. Since he has grown up, most of his memory is tabbed by the thought forms or the words associated with the event rather than the sensory impressions themselves. This seems to be the main reason for infantile amnesia, rather than the fact that life at an early age is too frightening or embarrassing or primitive, etc.

As time goes on we become more and more practiced at thinking in words. This, in turn, tends to affect our sensory awareness to the point where we very often only consciously perceive what the words tell us should be there. The extreme form of this type of behavior—where one only perceives what one is looking for or expects to perceive—is sometimes called senility. It is the result of years and years of being primarily aware of thinking in words and not paying attention to the fundamental nature of experience.

Dreams And The Senses

As I have said, we begin to become good at thinking in words by the time we are about five years of age. As this happens, we start to lose a lot of our freedom and responsiveness to nature. This is evidenced in the way children's drawings change from the magnificent free-form creations they produce at a younger age into the much more stereotyped ones they do once they have started in school. The words, and the emotions that go with them, build and build and build into the primary side of our awareness and thinking. At times we get all tangled up in these thought forms because we increasingly tend to ignore the more subtle and yet important messages coming to us from our senses. Then, when the day is over, we fall asleep and our consciousness is largely put aside. While we sleep, we cycle dreams past our remaining consciousness approximately every hour and a half. These dreams seem to be the end result of our mind's struggle with the imbalance in the data with which it is dealing. When the mind gets it sorted out, it tries to show us some of the distortions we are making in our reality by not paying attention to the more experiential level of awareness. Because of this lack of attention, this level of awareness is often forgotten. Yet it contains the data we need for a more balanced program of thought. Since the rules for this nonverbal type of thinking are different from verbal reasoning, it is a very different ball game from our conscious stream of thought. As a result, dreams are presented to us in a seeming jumble of symbols and feelings that initially are somewhat confusing to us upon awakening. However, underneath this jumble is a consistency that follows its own rules. They happen to be our own basic rules of thinking that have relatively little to do with language, other than the fact that words are incorporated in dreams too.

Because dreams are based on our own fundamental nonverbal thought processes, they have a haunting sense of meaning that makes it very hard for us to ignore the process altogether. Once we begin to understand it, we realize that dreams do indeed interpret for us the nature of the reality we are making for ourselves.

There you have it. Thought can be divided into at least two levels of function. The first is a sensory experiential level in which our senses inform us of what is going on around us and what is going on inside of us—and what our purpose and intent is. It is a level of functioning that serves us quite well during the first few years of our lives. Interestingly enough, it is this sensory development, rather than our verbal growth, that seems to engender the development of our I.Q.

The second level of thinking is in thought forms, most of which are words. The majority of us utilize this type of thinking consciously for most of our lives. Neither of these types of thinking is, in and of itself, good or bad. Where we get into difficulties is in the balance that occurs between them. Most of us tend to be overbalanced on the verbal thinking side of our nature and lose awareness of the more fundamental and more natural thinking that underlies this process. In any event, in the dream state we revert to this more fundamental type of thinking, perhaps guided by our soul to give us a better understanding of the nature of the reality we are making for ourselves.

It really is unfortunate that this communication tool we use so effectively with words turns out to be, in the long run, a limiting factor to our consciousness. We certainly can't get by without words. But when we rely too much on them, we end up limiting our awareness and lead lives that are not nearly as rich as they might be.

On the other hand, if we start to practice thinking without words, things begin to change. Try it some time. Most people are dismayed to discover that, at first, they can go only a few seconds without some form of words in their minds. But, with practice, the time gets longer and longer in the consciousness without the internal dialogue. As it does, we begin to experience ourselves and to become aware of things in us that we have only dreamed of before. As we gradually get our thinking back into better balance with this practice, life starts to assume the richness of feeling that is in our dreams and everything seems to go better.

At the same time, our dreams become brighter, more frequent and easier to understand. Because we are getting caught up with the purpose of ordinary dreaming and are thus free to go beyond it, our dreams occasionally take on the form of visions.

But until we reach this stage, the purpose of dreams and dreaming is to interpret the nature of the reality we are making for ourselves.

CHAPTER II

The Impact of Dreams on History

Less than 600 years ago, most maps of our earth were ornamented with sea monsters and unmarked jungles. There did exist, however, in some European libraries, a few maps that showed the shape of the world with considerable accuracy, including at least two of Antarctica. How these maps came into being and where they came from remains a mystery. Obviously there was somebody around a long time ago who really knew about the size and shape of the world and its continents.

The same kind of thing seems to be true for the study of human dreaming. Ancient literature is full of examples of dreams and their interpretation—and quite often the interpretation is extremely accurate according to the way we look at dreams today. Yet, for the last thousand years or so, dreams have been relegated to the area of superstition, and the books on the interpretation of dreams for this period are very, very bad. Much of what went on seems to have been pure charlatanism. This, of course, changed dramatically at the turn of the century when Sigmund Freud wrote his book on dreams. Since that time our understanding of dreams and dreaming has grown by leaps and bounds until, at the present, we have once again, I think, recovered most of the ancient understanding of dreams—except for one thing. In general, psychiatrists and psychologists have difficulty in dealing with the existence of the soul—something that in no way troubled the ancients. Despite this fact, however, modern day psychological science has made remarkable progress in understanding both the sleep state and the dream mechanism itself.

The earliest records available to us—Sumerian clay tablets scratched with cuneiform writing—tell about dreams and how they were interpreted.

On some of these tablets they discovered an epic poem telling of a hero king, Gilgamesh, and of his numerous battles, struggles, dreams and mystical experiences. An interesting aspect of this epic is that a portion of it parallels almost word for word the story of Noah as it appears in Genesis, except that Gilgamesh releases a crow instead of Noah's dove. The poem recites many of the dreams of Gilgamesh and his companions, including one from the night before a battle which had Gilgamesh concerned. In the dream Gilgamesh, with a group of friends, climbed to the top of a mountain. Suddenly the mountain fell under their feet and "they were as numerous as flies in the canebrake." He told his mother about it and she interpreted the dream as a good omen. She said it meant that he would achieve his aspirations and be victorious in the battle, represented by the mountain. Furthermore, it would be a crushing defeat for his enemies and he would attain numerical superiority, symbolized by the flies in the cane-brake. This interpretation parallels almost exactly the way this dream would be interpreted today, at least on one level. However, today's emphasis would be upon Gilgamesh's inner development.

The Egyptians believed that dreams had magical qualities and came from the gods or from the dreamer's soul and their manuscripts, like many ancient writings, gave directions for using dreams. The Torah and the Koran set forth rules for deciphering the meanings of dreams, as do Hindu and Chinese texts. Jewish literature abounds with dreams —from the familiar stories of Jacob's son, Joseph, to the flight into Egypt of the family of Jesus.

It is not surprising that reports of dreams are as old as human history. Laboratory research has revealed that dreams are an essential biological activity shared by all warm blooded animals. What is surprising is the skill which people like Joseph and Daniel used in interpreting dreams.

Subconscious Help In Problem Solving

It was the emotional intensity of dreams that first attracted man's attention. But what kept his attention (and what accounts for the writing of this book) was the usefulness of his dreams. He began to discover that he regularly dreamed about what he was most involved in and concerned about at the time. And the dream always contained a fresh viewpoint that was helpful in understanding the situation. It seemed to provide insights for solving problems that appeared unsolvable in the light of day. He was somehow presented with practical information not covered by his conscious knowledge or state of development. Frequently the dream seemed to predict events with considerable accuracy and surprising detail. As a result, man began to rely on his dreams for guidance in his life. Examples of this use of dreams can be found in ancient literature from all around the world.

Because of this wide range of usefulness at a time when man's tools for understanding his universe were limited, dreams were carefully studied and people were taught to interpret them. We are told that part of the training of Egyptian temple initiates was for them to be permitted to sleep until they awakened naturally. This way they were able to recall the night's dreams more vividly and discuss them with their teachers.

The ancients took their dreams more seriously than any of us are inclined to do today. There were exceptions, of course. Caesar and Pilate refused to heed the warnings of dreams—with tragic results. Most ancient people did pay attention to these strange occurrences in their sleep because they believed them to be divinely inspired. The wealth of references to dreams in early literature indicates just how seriously man took them and how hard he tried to understand them. These messages, which early man usually attributed to the gods or his soul, were no easier to unravel than are our dreams today. Modern dream analysis stresses that they are messages from within our being and that only the dreamer holds the key to understanding them. Both the ancient and current dreamer realized that one must study a dream carefully to extract all of its significance. The entire ancient world honored those who were able to explain the meaning of dreams.

Biblical Dream Interpretation

A familiar story is the Biblical account of Joseph, son of Jacob, who was sold into slavery in Egypt by his brothers. Although Joseph's master entrusted him with the care of his estate, the master's wife plotted against Joseph and he was thrown into jail in disgrace. While he was there he met two of Pharaoh's servants, the chief steward and the chief baker, who both had had dreams on the same night. Joseph interpreted the steward's dream about a vine with three branches to mean that in three days the Pharaoh would forgive him and restore him to his stewardship—and it came to pass. The baker was not so lucky. Several years later, the Pharaoh himself had his well-known dream about the seven fat cows and the seven lean cows, seven full ears of grain and seven withered ears. None of the court wise men could explain the dream. The steward remembered that Joseph, who was still in prison, had demonstrated an ability for remarkably accurate dream interpretation. Joseph was brought to the court where he told the Pharaoh that God had sent the dream as a warning that there would be seven years of plenty followed by seven years of famine. Surplus from the time of plenty should be stored to feed the people during the famine. It is recorded that the years of plenty and the years of famine came as the dream foretold. The Egyptians survived because, on the advice of Joseph, Pharaoh followed the wisdom of his dream.

An even more amazing account of interpretation is found in the story of Daniel. The Babylonian king, Nebuchadnezzar, wasn't sleeping well. His dreams were most disturbing. Yet when he awoke he couldn't remember what had happened in them—only that they had been quite troubling. He called in all his wise men and ordered them to not only interpret the dream, but to first tell him what his dream had been. The experts were horrified. This wasn't in their contract. No one, except God, could know what someone else had dreamed without being told. Nebuchadnezzar, in a royal rage, ordered all the wise men killed. Among the men for whom a warrant had been issued was Daniel, a young noble Israelite who had been brought to Babylon as a hostage and who was being educated in the king's court. When Daniel heard what had happened between the king and his experts, he asked if he could be taken to Nebuchadnezzar. Daniel prayed to his God. When he was presented to the king, he was able to tell the king what his dream had been and its meaning: there would be four successive kingdoms which would rise and fall until a fifth kingdom was built which would stand forever. Nebuchadnezzar fell on his knees before Daniel in amazement and made him ruler over the whole province of Babylon because he was a revealer of mysteries and obviously favored by God. The only other person I know of who was able to equal this feat of telling the dreamer the part of the dream he had forgotten and then interpreting it was a man named Edgar Cayce.

A Key To The Healing Process

The people of other nations made use of dreams perhaps even more than the Jews did. In ancient healing temples throughout the Mediterranean, dreams were used by those who sought to diagnose diseases. The dreams were used as part of the cure as well. A patient would go to the temple and spend some time in preparation—praying, meditating and fasting. He would then go to sleep, usually in front of a statue of the god. His dream would be carefully analyzed by the priests in hope that it would contain information about the patient's illness leading to a cure. This use of dreams presupposed that they came from divine sources and sometimes elaborate preparations were used to insure that the gods spoke clearly. Dream incubation like the above is being studied again now. It seems to be quite productive.

Dream books in China, Japan and India not only cataloged particular images, but also attempted to explain their source and function. They related dream images to balance and imbalances in the circulation of "chi," or energy in the body, and a disruption of this circulation which, in turn, caused poor health. Consequently, Chinese and Japanese physicians of long ago listened very carefully to the patient's dreams because they provided information that could be useful in making a diagnosis and designing a treatment. The Chinese also tried to classify different dreams according to the feelings which were part of them.

The Greeks Had A Word For It

The history of dream study is indeed part of the history of philosophy—of man's attempt to understand his own mind and soul. Although we are, in part, affected by oriental contributions, our relationship to our dreams has been determined largely by the development of European thought, starting in Greece where dreams constituted an integral part of their literature. A man named Democritus who fathered the atomic theory when he described atoms as little triangles, was also probably the first one to propose an idea similar to Carl Jung's theory of the universal unconscious. He stated that information in dreams penetrates the dreamer's body and enters into his consciousness by means of telepathy—clear indication that he felt dreams came from the dreamer's soul.

Socrates' attitude toward dreams was somewhat Freudian. He declared that the beasts of emotion and lust are released in the dreamer, whose intellect is no longer on guard in the state of sleep. His description is, in many ways, an accurate one for the dreaming state.

Aristotle was more rational and scientific in his approach toward dreaming. He wrote several books on the subject and organized dream study work into its first comprehensive form. Aristotle was concerned with the lingering tendencies of sensory impressions. He felt the purpose of the dream was, at least in part, to reorganize the sensory impressions of the day before. He sensed the ability of dreams to predict somatic events, such as illness, and was a forerunner of many modern dream interpreters.

Symbols And Superstitions

The next important contributor was Artimadorus, a Roman of the second century, who gathered together most of the material on dreams known in his time. He searched Egyptian, Arabic, Greek and other available sources and wrote a dream book which has survived to the present time. It was published in Latin and most other Western languages. Some of the books published today contain material taken directly from Artimadorus' work. He introduced the concepts of free association on dream symbols and he also proposed the idea that dreams and visions are infused into men for their advantage and instruction. He stressed the importance of working with dream symbols and emphasized that they were not to be considered as an ironclad unwavering code. Symbols with a universal meaning exist. But each dreamer places his own particular twist on the symbols he is using and very often dramatically changes what would pass for the standard interpretation of that particular symbol. He pointed out that puns and punning are frequently used in dreams, as is well known today.

These men, Democritus, Socrates, Aristotle and Artimadorus, were among the great thinkers who pondered the significance of dreams, and their writings have helped to shape our current theories. The popular understanding of dreams held by their contemporaries was considerably more superstitious. People believed that if a woman dreamed of giving birth to a cat she would have many children. If she dreamed of giving birth to a dog, she would have a boy. Popular interest created a market for dream books which were catalogs of specific symbols and their meanings. Some which have survived are filled with the sensationalist, careless superstitions of their day. Others have suffered at the hands of centuries of editors and translators or have lost their significance because the culture for which they had meaning has vanished. Those books weren't very different from some books available today which tell you how to decide what number to bet on if you have such and such a dream. All of these books fail to take into account the individuality of the dreamer. Artimadorus' warning that symbols had to be interpreted with a view to the biases of the dreamer didn't sift down to the masses.

After the fall of Rome came the Dark Ages—a time when western man seemed to immerse himself in unconsciousness . . . a winter's hibernation of the analytical mind . . . a time when fear predominated over reason. As far as we know, most people at that time treated dreams in a very superstitious manner. The teachings of the philosophers were forgotten.

Thinking minds surfaced on the shores of the Renaissance and man woke up to his possibilities as an individual. But dreams, which could have been a great aid, were often discredited because of the superstition that had been attached to them in the preceding centuries. Charlatans had entered the field of interpretation and played on the naivete of men and women. Most of the dream books that were available were facile, and their illogical explanations alienated the intelligent searchers of the day. Out of the Dark Ages man had brought raw material to analyze and digest and wean on. But dream interpretations were too ambivalent, too tainted with a magical association to be easily classified. As man began to sort his experience into the various branches of science, dreams got left in the "sort-later" pile.

The use of dream material for divination and sophistry fell to its nadir after 1750 as Western thought opposed it as irrational and unmaterialistic. Man's focus shifted away from subjective awareness, and dreams were devalued. The culmination of this trend came at the time Thomas Hudson wrote his book, *The Law of Psychic Phenomena,* which was published just before the turn of the century. This book made a significant contribution to understanding the nature of the subconscious mind and psychic phenomena. However, Hudson stated that dreams are merely the eructations from bad digestion and have no more meaning than that.

The Impact Of Dreams On Francis of Assisi

It was not dreams which had changed, but man's understanding of how to use them. Some scholars who could not satisfactorily explain to themselves the source of dreams chose to deny their significance altogether. Others felt the power of dreams and listened. One of my favorites, a man who used his dreams to guide his growth, was Francis of Assisi. He regarded his dreams regularly. He started out in life as the son of an upper-middle-class clothier and had a pleasant, happy youth. But as he matured, his life began to change. When he was wrestling with the problem of going off to war, he had a dream in which he was in his parents' home. Suddenly the scene changed to a much more sumptuous and elaborate residence filled with saddles, swords and other implements of war. In one of the rooms of this house was a beautiful woman who was intended for Francis. When he woke up, even though he felt the dream was basically good, he started to cry and couldn't understand his crying. This dream led Francis away from the type of life described in the surface of the dream. The dream advised Francis that he had within him strength of a spiritual nature and that he had a beautiful soul waiting to help him. Even though it appeared to be a good dream, indicating success in war, he was dismayed because he had enough insight to realize that it was indicating a potential for a great change in his life style.

Every time Francis got into trouble with the Church he would have a dream which helped or reassured him. The night before he was to see the Pope about a disagreement they had, he had a dream in which he was standing beside a large and impressive pine tree. In the dream he grew very tall, as Alice did in Wonderland. He was able to push the tree around whichever way he wanted. Francis understood from this that he would be able to sway the Pope to his own ideas.

At another time Francis was concerned about governing his Order. He had preferred to deal with each problem individually but there were now so many members that he could no longer get to them all. He had a dream in which he saw himself as a mother hen with so many chicks that some were starving. They were trying to pick up little crumbs and eat them. In the dream somebody said to him, "Make those crumbs into a Host, Francis. You can do it!" So he did this, and some of the brothers ate the Host avidly. Others didn't. Upon awakening from this dream, Francis took heart and went ahead and wrote rules for the Order. That is, he took all the individual situations and made them into general rules. Those brothers who followed the rules did well spiritually. Those who did not, did poorly. In general, more brothers benefited than not.

Descartes And Luther

Even when man could deny a divine source for dreams, he couldn't deny their reality. Dreams have an unsettling way of waking the most confirmed non-believer with their vividness. Those seekers who had integrity didn't discount what they couldn't explain and kept an open mind. Rene Descartes credited a dream with giving him the basis of his philosophy.

Martin Luther was concerned with dreaming—but in its negative aspects. He used to pray not to dream because he was obsessive/compulsive and never could figure whether his dreams were true or false, right or wrong. Rather than get caught up in a dilemma that might last for days, he preferred not to dream in the first place.

Many continued to attend to their own dreams and to be guided by them. But as a subject of serious study they were disregarded. Dreaming, like a neglected tool for self-development, had to wait for man to rediscover its usefulness. The Renaissance in Europe had reawakened Western Man to the value of individuals and of individual growth. It was Sigmund Freud who fitted the tool to the job.

The Freudian Era

Freud realized that dreams were the perfect vehicle for connecting the conscious and the unconscious mind. With a dramatic sense of timing, he waited until the beginning of a new century. In 1900 he published his most important work, *The Interpretation of Dreams.* Freud had prepared this book earlier, but felt that the entry into a new era would be a better time to unveil it.

Freud began to focus attention on dreams in a way that had not been taken seriously until that time. He stressed that a dream comes from the dreamer and concerns the world inside the dreamer more than the world outside. Freud based his theories on the ideas that dreams originate from the expression of infantile wishes. This was based on an incorrect definition of the unconscious mind and what it does. It would have been better to have said "infantile thought processes." In addition, Freud felt that the purpose of the dream symbol was to disguise the meaning of the dream rather than to convey information to the conscious mind because he considered most of its content to be sexual. He envisioned a censor that prevented dream information from entering into conscious awareness. I mention these ideas, even though many of them are currently falling into disrepute. We now take umbrage with the idea of a censor and have come to believe that symbols are used in dreams to convey information rather than to disguise it.

It is conceded that a dream might be an expression of a wish—but not exclusively an infantile or sexual wish. It can also be a wish to make oneself a better person or to solve whatever imbalance or problem exists at the time of the dream. Freud distrusted the unconscious and thought of dreams as symptoms of discomfort. He was really only a step beyond Hudson's bad digestion theory—but it was a major step because Freud internalized the disruptions. He understood that it was personal experience and frustration (not beans and cream pie) that made dreams bubble up. He was limited by his obsession with sexual repression and was unable to see that other frustrations might also arise from social, religious or even financial conflicts.

Jung Builds On Freud's Foundation

It was one of Freud's students, Carl Gustav Jung, who took the next step and discovered that dreams were related to all aspects of our lives —physical, mental, social, moral and material. He saw that dreams could plumb the depths of our souls, which led to his concept of the archetype and the collective unconscious. He realized that a dream was a statement as to the nature of our own reality, both subjective and objective, and what we made of it.

Jung pointed out that dreaming is a part of an internal balancing process maintained by every human being—that some of the things expressed in dreams, such as motives or the meaning of daily situations we have overlooked, are not consciously recognized. Consequently, emotions that we banished from our awareness and criticisms that we spared ourselves in our waking lives are reviewed for our benefit in our dreams. On the other hand, dreams can also be full of positive factors.

Freud could never accept Jung's theories. In his autobiography, *Memories, Dreams and Reflections,* Jung tells of a dream that he had which he asked Freud to interpret. In the dream Jung was in an elegant house which he knew to be his own although it was unfamiliar. He descended to the basement and found that the walls there were from Roman times—a discovery which excited him. He then uncovered a trap-door leading to a subbasement where two old skulls were partially buried. In interpreting the dream, Freud concentrated on the skulls, feeling certain that they represented a death wish for his father. Jung believed that the dream had more positive implications and realized that Freud, with his obsession with Oedipus, would be of little assistance in understanding it.

This dream was a turning point for Jung. It caused him to break away from the Freudian limitations. Freud's theory seemed to flow from the assumption that man is closest to perfection at birth and that life warps and corrupts the natural man. Jung implies the opposite: man is evolving toward a more perfect state, toward unity. He called this process "individuation"—the maturing of the self in each of us—and he saw that dreams were healthy messages stimulating growth in previously unexplored directions. Jung's contributions have led to our present understanding that dream study is a continuing education exploration. We can venture into strange dreams, motivated by the belief that dreams are for our own benefit. The aberrations we meet there can be disarmed with the affectionate attention of anyone who says, "What are you trying to tell me?" However, Jung's emphasis on the esoteric depths of the human psyche can lead to interpretations of dreams that miss the immediate and most positive impact of that particular dream experience.

Dreams In Action

During World War I, a German corporal fell asleep in his bunker in the front lines. He had a vivid, startling dream that an artillery shell made a direct hit on the bunker in which he was sleeping. He jumped up and ran out of the bunker which was immediately destroyed by an artillery shell. The man's name was Adolph Hitler.

General George Patton utilized his dreams regularly. A member of his staff reported to a friend of mine that Patton would retire early on the eve of battle—not only to insure adequate rest but to give him a better opportunity to dream about the coming day.

Dreams are still shaping history today. On October 16, 1970 a double-page ad appeared in TIME magazine describing a stretch of undeveloped woodlands in central Pennsylvania and advertising a fun-filled vacation there at a resort manned by the mentally retarded. The project was called Parklands Payback and it is taking place in several states. It is a dream come true.

Dan Torisky, the dreamer, is a 6'6" enthusiast, fully dedicated to his commitment. Several years ago Dan and his wife became interested in the study of dreams. One morning he woke up with a dream that seemed so important he stayed home that day to work it out. From the dream he got the idea for a recreation area located near a major highway in Pennsylvania's Parklands, to be staffed primarily by retarded workers. They would live in their own accommodations nearby and have ample opportunity to get around, go into town, etc. during off hours. It was a plan that benefited everybody. The state obtained money from private investors to develop unused parklands. The retarded have the dignity of a salary, social security and a life of fulfillment. And the patrons of the resort benefit from the vacation and recreational opportunities afforded there.

This same plan is taking place in several states for various categories of disability. It is very definitely changing the nature of reality for a lot of people who have been labeled developmentally disabled and whose lives have been generally empty and neglected until now. We are finally learning just how much a retarded individual can do if given the proper training and opportunity. There is no question they can do most of the jobs in a resort area and take care of themselves as well.

Now many of them are doing just that as the result of Dan's implemented dream.

Although Dan and his wife are parents of a handicapped son, Dan is in no way a professional in the field of developmental disabilities. He is president of a small marketing agency in Pittsburgh, Pennsylvania. The stuff of his dream, he quietly asserts, came from "somewhere beyond himself."

CHAPTER III
The Nature Of Dreams— The World Within Us

Man has persisted in the study of dreams throughout the ages—not only because dreams provide a wealth of information about our daily world, but especially because of what they tell us about our relationship to the world within us. This inner world contains the reality we are making for ourselves. In ancient times, interest in dreams centered around the possibility of receiving messages from the gods to help solve particular problems. Early records confirm this. Yet even then there were some wiser people who realized that dreams had a deeper significance and who raised questions as to their function in the growth of the personality. From our modern viewpoint, we believe that the majority of dreams are concerned with the world within the dreamer rather than with external events. We hold that dreams work as a mechanism within the dreamer to stabilize both mind and body, as well as to provide a running record of the inner development of the dreamer as a person. Current research gives us some fascinating insights into what the dream is and what it does, although science still doesn't know where dreams come from or why. What is important to us today, however, is that dreams give us clues to understanding how our minds work. We find the study of our dreams is an invaluable approach to self-development, because in doing so we are using a safe mechanism provided by nature with the checks and balances one always finds in natural processes.

The history of dream interpretation—of man's understanding of dreams—is the story of the internalization of the dream's *primary* significance. The content of dreams hasn't changed markedly over the centuries. No Egyptian ever told of dreaming about a drive in a new model Cadillac, but lots of Pharaoh's foot soldiers probably dreamed of riding in an unattainable chariot. While the content of the dreams that have survived in writing is not unfamiliar, the focus

Interpreting Your Dreams

of interpretation has changed. The god who placed that foot soldier in the chariot is now regarded as an aspect of the dreamer's higher self. Dreams have many layers of meaning and man has emphasized different layers at different times.

The nature of dreaming somehow makes it a one-man show that needs that same man to make the interpretation. That, of course, is the reason for books like this one—to help individuals who are really concerned wth their own dreams to make some sense out of them.

The study of your own dreams is well worth the effort. It is one of the simplest and most effective means of self-help that I know of. It uses a natural process and consequently is about as safe as any method can be. The people I know who have used this method with themselves have all changed very much for the better over a period of a few years.

Write It Down

The first rule in dream work is to record your dreams. The best way to record them is in written form, preferably in a notebook in journal fashion so that you can refer back to dreams of a previous month or year if you need to. It's nice to see the progress you are making, and this can only be done with a dream journal. Dreams also can be recorded in some other fashion, such as taping them. If, however, you do tape dreams, you must be willing to write them down later on. The best advice is to keep a notebook of some kind and a pen or pencil at your bedside for making notations of the dreams as they come. This is particularly true of dreams that come in the middle of the night. Many is the time that I have wakened from a vivid dream, spent some time thinking about it, and then gone back to sleep sure that I would be able to recall it—only to waken in the morning and not be able to bring that dream back into my memory. One other method of keeping a dream in mind is to tell it to somebody else. This might lead to some interesting interaction between bed partners, but it does work.

Analyze The Emotion

The second rule in working with your own dreams is to "run out" all the emotion. We waken from almost every dream with some kind of emotional feeling left over. These feelings may be positive, negative or neutral. They may be very strong or relatively mild. Regardless of what they are, they should be thought about, felt, associated to, and in general run out until they no longer seem to bother us. If you do nothing more than this with your own dreams, you will have done yourself a very great service.

Fishing For Truth

Those who have paid even more attention to their dreams have unearthed valuable insights. For example, a gentleman who was a beginning student of dreams had the following one during a vacation at the seashore in which he attended lectures on how to work with his dreams. He was standing on the beach fishing. With him was a small boy, apparently his son. He managed to catch two fish which he laid on the sand, intending for the boy to pick them up and take them home. However, a beaver and a rabbit came up and ate the fish before he could retrieve them.

He thought quite a bit about this dream and got some help from his class. He finally came up with the following interpretation which he felt was correct. The ocean represented his oceanic unconscious, a fount of spiritual knowledge in which he was fishing for truths—spiritual lessons—psychological insights—with which to help himself. And he caught them. These truths, or food for thought, were symbolized by the fish. The youngster in the dream was that growing but not yet matured aspect of himself involved in his interest and work along these lines of self-development. Incidentally, he had no children of his own. The beaver in the dream represented his work. He was a man who held two jobs and "worked like a beaver at them." The rabbit represented another aspect of himself. I don't think I have to go into some of the common terms we use about rabbits and their sexual behavior. The trademark of *Playboy* magazine gives us a clue. Although married, this man was a bit of a playboy. After putting all of this information together, it was perfectly obvious that the dreamer was telling himself: "Sure enough, while you are studying and working at these things, you are going to catch some truths, and these will be nourishing truths if you are able to use them. But if you are not careful, your excesses at work and in play are going to interfere with the learning and digesting of these truths even though you have caught them." He took the message to heart, quit his extra job, got rid of his mistress, and has grown faster in his self-development ever since.

The Lemon Juice Cure

Another example is a dream that a wife had for her husband. He had severe asthma that caused him a great deal of difficulty. One night the wife dreamed about her husband drinking lemon juice. They had tried practically everything else for the man's problem, so the wife suggested perhaps he should try the juice. For breakfast the next morning he had a glass of the lemon juice, uncut, which he seemed to enjoy. The condition almost immediately cleared up—and apparently as long as he stays on the lemon juice he is free of the asthma.

It's A Boy!

One day a patient of mine who was pregnant announced that during the past week she had had several dreams—one in which she saw a pot breaking and another in which something pink had been changed into something blue. I was able to sit back wisely and say, "Well, it looks like you are going to have your baby pretty soon." Of course, I didn't need the dream to tell me this since she was as big as a house. I then went on to say that it was probably going to be a boy. The lady had the baby the next day—and it was a boy. The reason for the change from pink to blue was that she had been hoping for a girl. The dream's purpose was to help prepare her for the birth of her boy by changing her attitude.

Faith Reborn

Another dream helped to heal an emotional wound. A mother, who had lost a child born with birth defects, was angry at God and at the world as well. One night she had an overpowering dream in which she saw the hand of God coming down to present her with a baby. Within a month she conceived a second child which was healthy—but, equally important, her faith in God was reborn. An interesting sidelight to this dream is that the second child is now entering adulthood and is showing signs of being a special person. Perhaps the dream was remarking on this as well.

Looking For The Right Valentine

The next example of dreams, and how they try to help, is a tragic one. I had a patient who had gone to a nationally famous clinic for a complete and thorough physical checkup before being sent to me. The clinic gave him a clean bill of health. However, they felt he had a very severe anxiety neurosis and recommended he see a psychiatrist. After I had been working with this man for about three months, he had the following dream. He was in a house of ill repute where there was a party in progress. There were different activities going on at the party, but he was not joining in them. Instead, he was standing at a little table off to the side of the room going through a large stack of valentines trying to find the right one. When I heard this dream, the events at the party that he related to me fit right in with the dynamics of his anxiety neurosis and were quite helpful in understanding this. But I couldn't understand the part about the valentines.

Three weeks later this man missed an appointment and I heard nothing from him. I was a little upset and concerned because the case had been going well, and this patient was conscientious and not one from whom I would have expected such behavior. Two weeks later, his daughter called and explained that the night before his scheduled appointment he had died in his sleep of a heart attack. Then, of course, this last part of the dream became clear. A valentine is, figuratively speaking, a report on the condition of your heart. He had been saying in the dream that he hadn't gotten the right report from the clinic. He was, unfortunately, correct.

The Designing Spider

Another interesting dream, and one that is also a bit tragic, was experienced by a man who changed jobs a few months after he had this particular dream. In the dream he was putting on a new coat when out of the sleeve came a large spider that started to attack him. He became frightened, got a knife someplace and started to slash at the spider—but he found that he kept cutting himself instead of doing much damage to the spider. The interpretation of this particular dream was that this man would be changing jobs and in the new work situation he would get involved with a designing woman—the kind who weaves all kinds of webs. The dream was warning him that if he didn't remove himself from this situation he could cause considerable damage to himself. He failed to heed the warning and did not disentangle himself from the woman soon enough. He eventually ended up making several suicide attempts.

These examples give you an idea of how dreams can be helpful with physical problems, material dilemmas and with mental and spiritual developments. These dreams are just a few of the ones that we have collected. They are not extraordinary ones. They come from a wide variety of people who are not especially gifted dreamers; ordinary people who are different only in what they were interested in collecting and understanding in their own dreams.

Can You Interpret Your Own Dreams?

There is some controversy in the field of psychology as to whether or not it is proper, or even possible, for the dreamer to interpret his own dream. Being a psychiatrist, this is a most important point to me. With Carl Jung and many others, I feel there is no question that, in the final analysis, the only interpretation of a dream that is really accurate must come from the dreamer himself. There are nuances that appear in dreams—the shades of color and feelings that can't possibly be communicated to someone else. There are also association links that nobody else knows of or has. As a result, any interpretation that another person might make of your dreams, even though it can be helpful, is not going to be as full as the interpretation and understanding that can eventually come from you. The nature of the dream process is such that an outsider can usually only comment rather than be directly involved.

Some psychologists even say that it is dangerous for an individual to interpret his own dreams. Occasionally I have seen individuals develop mild psychological difficulties from learning too much about themselves too quickly through dream material. However, the only times I have seen this happen have been when somebody else made the interpretation rather than the dreamers themselves. If you are going to be interpreting your own dreams, your mechanisms of defense will keep things going at the right pace so that you don't have to be apprehensive about learning things too quickly.

It is important that dreams be approached with self-confidence. They are your productions and a living part of yourself. How you feel affects your utilization of the material presented. It may even affect the interpretation itself. Much of the symbolic material in dreams is two-sided, like a coin, and many symbols can be taken as "either-or." Consequently, working with a sense of confidence allows you to see the positive side clearly.

The Meaning Of Murder

As an example, let us take a simple dream which a young woman found most disquieting. In the dream she murdered her sister. She found this very upsetting because she had an intense hatred and jealousy for her sister. She therefore interpreted it to mean that she wished her sister dead and that she might actually take her sister's life. With further reflection, however, she realized that, in addition to warning her about her emotions and about controlling them, at a deeper level the dream was going one step further and suggesting that she "kill off" her negative attitudes towards her sister. At an even deeper level, the dream was trying to show her that she had deep-seated, self-centered resentments towards all of her "sisters"—all feminine competitors.

Get The Inside Story

A dream is a message from you to yourself. Your body's biologic cycles provide a place in the flow of time when such a message can be transmitted. This happens about every 90 minutes during the time that you are sleeping. The content of that dream production is up to you. You make up the dream from start to finish. The events of the day may suggest symbols to you—particularly what you experience 90 minutes before falling asleep. Nobody else can weave the dream together to fit just you and your reality. You choose the theme. You write the plot to express that theme. You select the images which will clothe the story and add overtones of meaning as well as identifying the characters. You give the hero a white hat or a black hat. You paint the scenery to create a mood. You select the characters and give them their lines. The research described in the following chapters suggests that you are also the production engineer who gets it all recorded before the curtain rises. The technique is so advanced, however, that if a chandelier falls during the performance or an alarm clock rings it is incorporated into the play.

The show opens to an expectant audience—you. You play your part as audience so well that you pretend to forget that you know what it is all about. Sometimes your attention strays and you miss scenes that you can't recall the next day. Other times you become distracted by the leading lady or shocked by the villain and forget the lessons which the theme was intending to convey.

To study dreams and extract their full value you must also play the part of the drama critic whose livelihood depends upon sensitive deciphering of the playwright's deepest intentions. The playwright chooses the theme and the images that spring from his feelings. The critic must savor the subtle artistry which selected these images, while he uses his intellect to rediscover the theme and put it into words. Sometimes the critic discovers layers of significance of which even the author was unaware.

One of the characteristics of dreams that differentiates them from other states of consciousness and from the psychic phenomena that occur during sleep is that dreams have a familiarity even when they are exciting or disturbing. If you think about the events that took place in the dream sequence, it becomes obvious that what you see or experience in a dream never takes you entirely by surprise. Your attitude is very much the same as it would be in any theatrical performance. When you choose a movie or a play, you do so with some idea of what it will be like and what is going to happen. Consequently, as the events unfold in the movie or in the dream they have a familiar appropriateness.

Occasionally you may have a dream which is more like a news flash —direct from the control room. Psychic experiences during sleep, which we will examine in a later chapter, take one by surprise and just don't seem to fit in with the rest of the evening's production. This is one way of spotting the psychic experiences which do happen from time to time during dreaming. It takes practice and experience to get good at telling the difference.

A Message From Your Subconscious

A dream is an attempt of the subconscious mind to convey information to your conscious awareness. Sometimes dreams are presenting information we would rather not hear. As we go through life, we form certain convictions and opinions about ourselves. In other words, we make our own reality. These convictions are unrealistic when we emphasize our virtues and minimize our vices or when we emphasize any part of our character that keeps us from growing and developing fully. It is a common human failing to be blinded to our weaknesses because they don't fit with our need to be what we think we should be. In fact, any weakness in our character, any neglected area of growth, is a blind spot in our vision of ourselves. Dreams can hold up a mirror to show us our flaws or our beauty and thus help eliminate our blind spots and aid in our development.

We are sometimes disinclined to admit that we are not as good as we think we are. It is just this message that our dreams are frequently trying to point out to us because it is information that we really do need to know.

It is difficult to confess to ourselves that we eat too much, that we really should see our family doctor about our blood pressure or that we might even have to go to the hospital and have a kidney stone removed. These physical concerns are a bother and easy to put off until tomorrow. But if we avoid our responsibilities long enough, we may have more trouble as time goes on. Dreams insist that we pay attention. They are as cunning as the mother who tells stories to her two-year-old child about the vegetable soup she is trying to spoon in. Dreams also convey warnings about dangerous behavior. They may be trying to remind us that we really are much too selfish for our own good by having us buy so much stuff at the store we can't carry it. Or a dream in which we are chased by giants might be a reprimand for frightening the children. Sometimes they give us graphic descriptions of what might happen if we continue to hate our brothers. At other times they encourage us to keep on loving.

We are often like a man whose foot has been asleep so long he forgets how it feels. It may hurt a little when the feeling returns, but if he doesn't get that part back into circulation, it will begin to decay. Our dreams tickle us to remind us of sleeping parts of ourselves and to remind us of our "response-abilities." But, of course, all the messages in dreams are not negative. A dream can be an encouragement, telling us to keep up the good work of developing our strength in love. A dream can be a pat on the back, an Honor Day assembly program. They may be composed to reassure us and urge us to keep on going until we round a corner and come out of the shadow into a brighter time.

Dreams always tell us things we need to hear, but these messages do not have to be unhappy. They can and do give us pleasant insights that we would like to know. For many of us, it is even more difficult to hear that we are good than that we are bad. Years of underestimating ourselves may have left us reveling in our self-deprecation. Dreams can open a window on stuffy inhibitions or bring in the affection needed to melt blocks of fear. I know people who wake up laughing at times.

Dreams can wake us up with the joy of living when they tell us that we are doing all right or that if we keep going a change will occur that will result in a happy ending.

What Is Reality?

Whether we have been overemphasizing our virtues or our vices, if our self-view is unrealistic we had to go through a real struggle to establish it in the first place. It sounds quite easy to say, "Well, I can kid myself into thinking this or that." You may be able to kid yourself now, but you really had to work at it and practice it for years and years before it got to be so easy. When you were a child, you took things literally. You didn't understand about extenuating circumstances and it wasn't easy to find excuses. To form an unrealistic opinion of yourself, you had to expose yourself to some force that would push and push you out of shape to convince you either that you were invincible or that you were worthless. This began to happen when you shifted your level of thinking from the experiential into the thought forms which we now call language.

The world provides ample opportunities for all of us to see ourselves as both fallible and fine. We all fall into those traps of self-pride and self-pity and develop attitudes that are unrealistic and complicate our relationships with people. Dreams will expose these attitudes in all of their endless permutations and combinations. They are very good at showing us the futility of selfishness.

A New Way Of Thinking

Sometimes we must give up old habits and allow for a new expanded order in our lives. But we are not always overjoyed at the prospect of giving up familiar ways of thinking. I don't suppose a bird about to emerge from a shell is all that excited about its struggles either. But when it has ingested all the nutrients stored within its old shell and has grown to fill its limits, some inner prompting directs it to break out. Dreams provide us with our own inner prompting.

Because we had to work hard to build our self-images, we cling to them with the same desperation with which we would cling to our clothing if someone tried to strip us in public. If our convictions are pulled from us too suddenly, we would be even more upset than if we were stripped naked. It is easier to find some kind of clothing or covering than it is to find a new set of convictions or framework to support us mentally. These self-images have been endeared to us by their familiarity. We panic if we are suddenly without them and tend to hang on to them like an old pair of jeans. They are some of the difficulties we struggle against when we begin to study our dreams.

The study of dreams is complicated by our resistance to change. The purpose of this study is to make our growing easier and swifter. But the struggle to grow creates change and a fight against our own resistances. It is a bit like doing isometric exercises—pushing one hand against the other to build up strength. When we begin to work with our dreams, we bring the resources of our conscious mind to the effort to know ourselves better and establish a realistic self-view—a view in harmony with all the forces within and without ourselves.

The Use Of Symbols In Dreams

To make it possible for us to receive the insight we need, dreams present their messages in symbols which express what we have no words for. Dreams are like parables in the Bible. Or perhaps it would be more appropriate to say that parables in the Bible are like dreams. It is no coincidence that Christ used this form for teaching. It is a method that is as old as mankind—even older than mankind, since dreams occur in animals as well.

To understand the parable or the dream, we have to be willing to work at it. One of the primary beauties of the dream in symbol form is that, if we want to understand it, we have to be willing to think about it, work at it, puzzle over it, ask other people's opinions about it and keep thinking about it. As we turn it over in our minds, we can savor its subtleties of feeling and explore its hidden facets. It isn't just handed to us on a silver platter. Anything we gain through our own efforts has an added value because of what we have put into it. The information thus gained is more precious and is consequently used more carefully. The dream is also presented in symbols to provide a safeguard. These self-views, as I mentioned before, are as essential to our functioning as our clothing. It would be rather difficult for me to work as a doctor without any clothes on. Similarly, without my own convictions about myself, I'd be in trouble.

Symbols that are trying to convey information which may be contrary to what we think about ourselves bring the information to our conscious awareness in such a way that if we do not wish to know or use it, it's not going to bother us. If we are not interested in trying to understand it, it's not going to bother our conscious mind that much. One can get up and say, "I had this curious dream last night," and by lunchtime have forgotten it. It presents the picture, but doesn't force us to pay attention if we are not ready. If we ignore the message long enough, our dreams may begin to drop stronger and stronger hints until we see it. But by then, we have been prepared by the earlier dreams. For others of us, our interest in the cares of the world may distract us until that dream stops being conscious. For even others, our hearts are so hardened that the new view of reality can't take root and grow (like the rocky ground in the parable). When we approach it with the right attitude and try to begin to understand it, a dream symbol will cease being bothersome when we solve its riddle and heed its lesson.

The dream is in symbolic form for yet another reason. When we are asleep, only a small amount of our conscious awareness is available and we cannot easily handle large quantities of data. The symbol is an ideal way to compress the maximum amount of information into the fewest data units. One picture is worth the proverbial thousand words —and a dream is a whole picture book.

A Reflection Of Our Attitudes

As I said before, the attitude with which we approach our dreams after awakening is of importance. If we are feeling fearful, we might see a flower as a tiger lily or a Venus-flytrap and be more frightened. If we are feeling confident, we might be able to recognize that the tiger in a dream is a regal beast and a symbol of nobility within ourselves. This is why it is so important to first "run out" the emotion left over from a dream before working with the symbols. Dreams are in symbols not just to safeguard us but also to intrigue us with their imaginativeness, humor and artistry. Just how long can anyone resist a really good story, even if it is a scary one!

To further entice us, dreams have different levels of meaning. They are like ancient temples—with outer courts for the masses and inner sanctuaries for the initiated. Anyone with a little faith can enter the outer courts, but one must work and study before one can enter into the place which houses the central mysteries that sanctify the temple and give it its deepest meaning.

Manifest And Latent Levels Of Meaning

Every dream has at least two basic levels. These are called the manifest and the latent content. The level of the dream which is presented to our senses is the manifest content. The silly things we see—the events, the sounds, the costumes, the characters—which don't necessarily make much sense but which are clearly there, are all manifest content. The manifest content sprouts above the surface. Buried below is a hidden system of associations which connect the exposed and at times seemingly unrelated things and events. The manifest content, however, has much information in it about the dreamer's way of thinking.

The underlying meaning which the dream was created to express is called the latent content. Latent means "that which exists but is as yet concealed or unrevealed." This latent content lies hidden beneath the surface waiting for a dedicated searcher. It is like a geologic seam of gold which lies beneath the earth. It shapes and supports the land forms above it. In some places it is deeper down and in other places it breaks out into the open. As we work with our dreams, like a prospector who studies the land forms of an area until he can tell where gold will be found without digging too deep, we come to be able to identify the symbols that appear when the latent gold of significance is close to the surface. The process of interpreting is like digging out the gold—bringing the latent content to the light.

There is much to be gained, however, from an examination of the manifest content alone. Geographical formations are beautiful and fascinating in their own right, quite apart from the buried gold they may hide from us. They show us about the effects of weather and water and they support a skein of life over the bones of the earth's structure. The manifest content of a dream tells a great deal about the current personality of the dreamer and his way of thinking. They may be removed from the action and merely be a spectator. They may be a helpless victim of circumstances. They may see things in black and white only, rather than in vivid color. They may go directly to the point or go "all 'round Robin's barn" before they get there. They may face their problems all alone or have lots of allies. All this is easily seen in the manifest content.

Choosing Our Symbols

The symbols we choose may ring like silly giggles or clash against our consciousness with hammer strokes. It is this slippery, lively, unconfinable nature of symbols which makes dream interpretation so frustrating and so fascinating. It is hard to pin down what a symbol is without killing its vitality. We use symbols daily in our conversations with each other. When we try to describe something or somebody, we very often say, "Well, it's like such and such." If we were trying to teach someone about the art of conversation, we might say that it is like a game of ping pong. One has to keep hitting the conversational ball back and forth. To tell someone about the latent content of dreams we have said that it was like a seam of gold. With these analogies we try to convey to others the feeling of some experience or thought—and an analogy is one use of symbols. We try to find some common familiar picture that is similar to the idea we want to share.

As things get more complicated and we try to talk about philosophical ideas or deep religious thoughts, we talk almost exclusively in symbols. To express purity we may say that it is like candle light. Of course, the similarity is elusive and difficult to see, but, nonetheless, there is some connection in the minds of most of us between a flame and the idea of purity. Some spiritual concepts can only be expressed with symbols. Buddhist monks draw circular mandalas to try to convey some of the ideas of God. Thus, when we get into very deep thoughts and spiritual understandings, almost all of the language we use is symbolic. As Carl Jung pointed out, we use symbols to give us ways of expressing and handling ideas or concepts that we don't clearly understand yet in words.

We also use symbols to express sensory information for which we have no exact words. One friend told me that living downwind from a sausage factory was like being inside a pair of old tennis shoes. With this, he gave me a most distinct impression of his experience—and yet did not express it in specific words.

Similarity Or Contiguity

Symbols mean more than words because they carry a variety of associations. The human mind primarily makes association in two ways: by similarity or by contiguity. By similarity, the mind recognizes that two seemingly different ideas have something in common. Grass and emeralds are connected by their green color. Grass and hair are connected because they both waft in the breeze. Words that sound similar can stand for one another as they do in a pun. Sometimes the similarity may be hard to see at first, but that makes it more challenging.

Things are associated by contiguity when they are found together—bread and butter, ocean and shore. They may be located side by side in place, which is a physical contiguity; or they may happen at the same time, which is a temporal contiguity.

These two concepts have parallels in other areas. There are two kinds of magic—symbolic magic and sympathetic magic. To work symbolic magic, one draws pictures or makes things which are similar to the people and concepts involved in the particular spell. In sympathetic magic, the spell is done by using something which has been contiguous with the individual on whom the spell is worked. A piece of hair will do, or an article of clothing. The most powerful magic combines the two. A magician making a voodoo doll might work fingernail trimmings from his proposed victim into the doll's body.

An example of similarity association in a symbol would be a valentine representing a report on the state of the dreamer's heart. An example of contiguous association in dream symbolism would be a necktie representing the dreamer's aorta or hair representing the dreamer's thoughts.

A third way that the mind makes association is the trickiest of all. Sometimes an image stands for its opposite! Being happy and not being happy can both be concerned with happiness.

Look Beyond The Obvious

When we are interpreting a symbol, we can't stop with the obvious. A symbol is a representation that doesn't aim at being a reproduction. If we are going to tell somebody about a lion, there is no sense in dragging in the lion—and a lot of sense in leaving the lion where it is! We can use the symbols rather than reproduce in its entirety the thing that we are describing. The symbols we use can do more than outline the actuality we wish to describe. If we choose imaginatively, we can convey even more about the lion in the telling than we could with a live lion. Symbols can express all that lion-ness has ever meant. One old lion in a cage (we certainly wouldn't bring in a wild, lordly lion) doesn't say nearly as much as the British royal crest.

A symbol is defined as something that represents more than itself. The roots of the word "symbol" mean to throw together or to put things together. A royal crest showing a lion weaves together all that "lion" means and all that "king" means, and it is even more full of significance than either one alone. The interweaving nets of associations which catch the meaning of our intentions are made in the ways we have already mentioned—by similarity, contiguity and occasional opposites.

Bridging The Gap

The symbols in dreams span the gap between the thought world and the world within the dreamer. They are like fibers in a woven bridge that connects two sides of a chasm so deep that misty clouds obscure the stream and land below. The two sides—thinking and being—are, of course, joined at the bottom of the valley. They are really the same land form—but to facilitate travel, a bridge is constructed above. The events inside and outside of our minds are both part of the same ground, but they are joined far below the level of our conscious mind. Up in our minds, dream symbols connect the two sides, the external and the internal world, and enable us to cross.

A dream is primarily a message about the reality of the world within us. It starts where we are. To travel across the bridge it creates, we must realize that it starts with us and ends with us. It is not about some external world unconnected to us. This is a very important concept to comprehend early in the business of working with dreams. A dream can be about things that seem to be going on outside us, but it is always primarily about what is going on inside us and our relationship to what is outside us. It is rare in working with human beings to say "always" or "never," but I believe it is justified here. Once in a while we may get a direct message about somebody else, but that doesn't mean the dream isn't about us too. It is tempting for all of us, when we have a dream, to interpret it as an E.S.P. flash. Then we can rush out and tell our dear friend that he is going to have an accident next week or that he shouldn't go to the senate tomorrow. To find precognitive information in dreams can be fun. It gives us a sense of power and control by showing that at least some part of us does know what's going on. But, if we stop there, we don't get our dream's worth. If we approach a dream as if it were something going on outside, we will miss the real message. The dream is most beneficial when we can accept that it is about the world within. We cannot make a proper interpretation of a dream if we fail to realize that it is primarily about what is going on within us at a physical, mental or spiritual level.

Isolating A Symbol

Let us give an example at this point of the things we have been discussing. I want to give you another illustration of a symbol in a dream and of how it can and should be approached. Suppose you had a dream in which you saw the man who lives next door. We will not consider a whole dream at this time but just one character who is a single symbol in the dream. In the interpreting of the dream you may decide that this symbol of the neighbor represents something that is close to you, but it doesn't represent the man who actually lives next to you. Most of the time dreams speak figuratively, not literally. The neighbor represents an aspect of yourself that is close to where you really live but is not exactly you as you think of yourself. He may represent some aspect or feeling that is close to the center of your being, some feeling in your own heart that is closely related to you. The particular feeling that he represents will be suggested by the context around the symbol in the dream. If in the dream you are afraid of that man next door, then he may symbolize something in yourself that you fear. If you are glad to see him in the dream, he may represent some pleasure near to your heart.

Let us look more closely at this symbol of the man next door. What kind of man is the real fellow who lives across the fence? The dream may use him to symbolize something which is connected to his actual job. Suppose the man who lives next door is a physicist. Instead of symbolizing by contiguity something that is close to you, he may symbolize something by similarity. Because he is a physicist, he may represent your attitude about advanced education or perhaps about the natural sciences. It all depends on what the real man next door means to you. He may suggest the respect and deference you feel for the understanding of natural forces. If, in your dream, you distrust this neighbor who is a physicist, it may mean that you distrust your own scientific method of solving problems.

Perhaps, in addition to being a physicist, the man next door is a playboy. If, for you, that is his most obvious characteristic, then this may be what you use him to represent. He may then be a symbol for your attitudes about social mores. He may especially represent those feelings that affect you closely. From this example I think you can see that any symbol, character or particular part of the manifest content of a dream can be understood as representing several different ideas, depending on what that character or event means to you at the time.

I want to emphasize that a symbol changes its meaning for you as you go through life. What it means to you at the time of the dream is, of course, the most significant. At one time you might think that being a playboy physicist is great and at other times you may not, depending on how you are wheeling and dealing yourself. I think you can see, with just one symbol, how two or three interpretations could reasonably be derived. The correct interpretation can only be chosen by you when you recall what that symbol meant to you as the dream was composed.

Very often there are two or three levels of meaning in a dream. A whole book has been written about one dream as the author dug deeper and deeper into its ramifications. In our illustration of the dream about the man next door, there might be a level of interpretation pertaining to your degree of education in the school of life, and there may be another level of interpretation, also applicable, concerning your attitude about the morality of being a playboy. These interpretations could both be valid and helpful and might interlock so that each one would help you to understand the other more accurately.

Symbolic Or Emblematic

The things which are part of a dream's manifest content are not always to be taken as symbols. Sometimes instead of being symbolic they are emblematic. Those things termed emblematic are representations of static conditions or objects in the material world. Those referred to as symbolic are of a living, breathing nature that conveys the real meaning of an experience to the dreamer. Basically the difference is that symbols mean more than what they represent and emblems mean less. If you saw an adding machine in a dream it could be an emblem for your business, a shorthand notation for a job that fit within definite limits and didn't change. A stethoscope labels a dream character a doctor. If the adding machine were a symbol it might represent attitudes about our numbered society or about how our life is adding up, but in an accountant's dream it might simply be an emblem for his work.

The symbols and their interactions are what dreams are made of, so that in working with our dreams these are two of the main things we must look at. What do the symbols represent about, or within, the dreamer? And what is the message of their interaction in the dream?

CHAPTER IV

The Bio-Mechanics of Dreams

Until the last decade, man could only guess about the geography of dreams guided by jumbled memories. Many people alleged that they didn't dream at all and for them the mystery of sleep was complete. However, in the last ten years reports have been coming back from scientists watching night after night over the machines which monitor sleeping experimenters. Their startling discovery is that we all dream —that all warm-blooded animals dream. For a variety of reasons we may forget our dreams, but they are there in profusion. Furthermore, dreams seem to be essential to our well-being, acting as a balancing mechanism to achieve an equilibrium of physical and mental health. The soundings affirm that there is something there to explore and that it's related as much to our biology as it is to our psychology.

Understanding The Nature Of Sleep

Since dreaming is defined as an event that occurs only in sleep, to understand the process of dreaming we must understand the nature of sleep. It is odd that man has for so long taken sleep for granted. Our early forebearers thought of sleep as a little death. Sometimes they called it the valley of the shadow of death, but civilized man rarely hesitates to drift off to unconscious vulnerability. We have spent a third of our history suspended in the unknown, and yet it is only now that Western science has begun to focus its attention on the study of sleep. Some of the discoveries seem self-evident. Others lead scientists to surprising glimpses of the workings of the mind.

Sleep is necessary to maintain life. We can go longer without food than we can without sleep. Our body's first need is for air. Water is the second most critical requirement. The third is sleep. Why sleep is so essential remains unanswered. Many of the reparative and restorative processes that occur during sleep can be accomplished just as well while we are resting, but there must be something vitally important about this activity which, even today, is not entirely understood.

Some suggest that our need for sleep may be psychological or a habit deeply ingrained by the eons which preceded the invention of the electric light bulb. But the studies of Nathaniel Kleitman revealed that, although there are night people who function best when most of us are asleep, and although some rare individuals live on a minimum amount of sleep, the basic patterns of all cultures, from the arctic to the equator, include five to eight hours of sleep out of every twenty-four, usually at night. Even if they allow for a siesta, all cultures have this long period of sleep.

Effects Of Sleep Deprivation

Although scientists don't yet clearly understand the beneficial rebalancing process of sleep, they have observed the disastrous effects of prolonged sleep deprivation. Keeping a man awake continuously has long been recognized as a simple and effective form of torture for extracting confessions. During the 1950's, volunteers underwent periods of wakefulness in sleep laboratories. The effects varied in intensity, but everyone suffered perceptual distortions as time went on, and the experiments raised questions about the psychological effects of staying up for protracted periods of time.

The ordeal of one wakeful volunteer, Peter Tripps, is described in the United States Department of Health, Education and Welfare's Report on sleep and dream research. Tripp attempted to stay awake for 200 hours, attended by physicians and psychologists, as a benefit attraction for the March of Dimes. He began to hallucinate after 48 hours—seeing cobwebs on his shoes and caterpillars crawling all over one of his observers. After 120 hours he imagined that a fire was blazing in a dresser drawer. Solving simple mathematical problems became an agonizing struggle as the days passed. By the end of eight days, he was suffering acutely from the delusion that the doctors had made him the victim of a sadistic conspiracy. After 200 waking hours, he fell into a 13 hour sleep. When he awoke, the most extreme symptoms had fled, but it wasn't until three months later that he recovered from a mild depression which began at the end of the experiment.

Sleep Is Active—Not Passive

One of the most important discoveries of the sleep researchers is the observation that sleep is a very active process. It is not the passive, completely restful stretch that it had been thought to be. Waking activities put a far greater drain on the body reserves and the musculature, but sleep is really a complicated process, particularly for the brain and the central nervous system.

Experimenters in Chicago proved that the amount of oxygen consumed by the brain while we are sleeping is at times essentially the same as the amount used while we are awake. This, incidentally, is not an easy experiment to perform. Reliable results were obtained from only one-third of the 20 subjects. If you can imagine how difficult it must have been to sleep with a bunch of tubes and needles in the veins and arteries of one's neck, you will have some idea of the difficulties which confronted the subjects and the experimenters. Just what the brain is doing is not yet clear, but at least it is busy with activities that are apparently necessary to maintain life.

It has been observed that during sleep the body recycles the key chemical used to transform food into energy that is used by the body cells. Studies at the LaFayette Clinic show that after four days without sleep the body will have used up its supply of this chemical called ATP. After four days, people who have been deprived of sleep begin to have symptoms—blurred vision, personality changes and experiences similar to delirium—which are often observed in cases of mental illness. When they were allowed to sleep, their bodies immediately began to take a chemical compound, which had accumulated during wakefulness, and turn it back into ATP. When they awoke, they approached normal behavior.

Other physical changes were easily observed in sleepers. Their blood pressure fluctuated. Sometimes there were small movements in their muscles—or their arms and legs twitched. Occasionally you could hear some vocal noises as if they were trying to talk but couldn't get it out. It was especially noticeable that several times each night they would begin to move their eyes behind closed lids in a rapid, erratic fashion as if they were watching a movie. All these changes seemed to happen simultaneously.

From electroencephalograph reports and laboratory observations, a pattern began to emerge. Sleep is not a homogenous blackout. Rather, it runs through cycles of different kinds of activity.

Identifying The Cycles Of Sleep

All biological activities occur in cycles. Some of these cycles, such as a single nerve impulse, take a tenth of a second. Others take a year to complete. And there are many, many cycles in between, such as the heartbeat and the menstrual cycle. More subtle periodicities affect us also. Most people's body temperature rises and falls a degree or two every day. We are most alert during the day when our temperature is highest. It falls off at night, and our deepest sleep coincides with the lowest temperature. This pattern, called the circadian rhythm, is one of our most stubborn characteristics.

Identifying the cycles of sleep was a major breakthrough. Although what pulls these tides of sleep remains a mystery, scientists have established that there are four distinctly different stages which repeat approximately every 90 minutes or so. Each stage has its characteristic brain wave pattern and signs.

In Stage I, we start with a light sleep and then gradually, during the first 45 minutes or so, go into what looks like a deeper sleep which is called Stage IV. In Stage IV all of our body activities follow very slow, regular, rhythmic patterns. From this we re-emerge back up into a light sleep. During the descent from Stage I to Stage IV, our body slows down and it becomes more and more difficult to awaken us. When we are in Stage IV sleep, everything goes back and forth in a slow, easy but fairly wide swing. Our brain waves show that we remain attentive to noises around us, but if we are awakened we don't easily remember being aware of these sounds or of dreaming. Even our eyeballs move slowly during this stage of sleep, sweeping back and forth diagonally.

Deep sleep may be a somewhat misleading term. We relax and sink a little further into the mattress and we don't respond as quickly to stimuli, but it may not be any "deeper" than any other stage. It is more accurate and scholarly to refer to it as Stage IV. After about 90 minutes, we begin to show a change in our physiologic balance and our brain waves show a pattern that is similar to, although not quite the same as, when we are awake. It is then that our eyes begin to move rapidly and erratically as though we are watching something. These rapid and random eye movements alerted researchers to recurring sleep cycles. This stage of sleep is called R.E.M., meaning rapid or random eye movement sleep.

R.E.M.—The Dream State

Researchers discovered that if they waited until the sleep experimenters' eyes began to move rapidly and then awakened them at the end of this stage, the sleepers would report vivid dreams. If they were awakened when they were not in R.E.M. sleep, they either couldn't remember any dreams or their recollections were vague and fragmented. From these findings, scientists deduced that it was primarily during R.E.M. sleep that we dream. Then it became very easy to determine whether or not a person was dreaming and the amount of time spent in the dreaming state. We just have to look at them in a subdued light. The cornea of the eyeball makes a distinct bump on the closed eyelid. We can watch this bump move around in rapid erratic fashion when they are dreaming. It moves in a slow rhythmic fashion when they are not. While observing a sleeping individual, you will find that they are usually motionless while in Stage IV sleep. If awakened at this time, they will record either no dreams or very fleeting snatches of dreams. When they enter into dreaming sleep, the entry is usually announced by what is called a gross body movement. In other words, they will shift their position in the bed or roll over—some movement that involves the entire body. Then we can observe the eyeballs beginning to move in a rapid erratic fashion. During the dream the individual may have minor body movements of one kind or another, such as hands or feet twitching a little bit, and occasionally some vocal noises. The dream is usually ended with another gross body movement. These are not invariable occurrences but this is the classic pattern of a sleeping, dreaming individual.

Cycles Continue When We Are Awake

Another interesting discovery showed that the hour-and-a-half dreaming cycle seems to continue even when we are awake. This is a brand new concept and it opens the door on all kinds of explorations. It appears that the cycle (a 90 minute fluctuation of mental attentions) is at a subsurface level even when we are awake. It is not apparent and doesn't interfere with what we are doing. This seems to explain why at various times of the day we may find it easier to sink into a reverie and why we sometimes can have a long, involved vivid dream during a half-hour nap. If we happen to catch the cycle at just the right time, we will spend most of the nap dreaming rather than in some other kind of sleep. There are also some indications that this cycle may have something to do with the occurrence of hallucinations in those individuals who are suffering from a psychosis. But a psychotic hallucination is not just the brakes being taken off the dream mechanism while we are awake. It is more complex and not clearly understood at the present time. We do know, however, that in people who are suffering with depression, the cycles of sleep are all out of kilter.

The Purpose Of The Shunt

If all of our body moved the way our eyeballs do, we would certainly be engaged in vigorous activity during some of our dreams. I remember having the very disquieting experience of falling asleep in class one day and starting to dream that I was running a steeple chase. I woke up to find myself running in my chair—which caused a minor sensation in the class. This story illustrates a point that if the rest of our body engaged in the activity of the dream the way our eyeballs do, it would wake us up and disturb our sleep—and that wouldn't help unless you are trying to stay awake in class. Some sort of mechanism is needed to shut off the nerve impulses to our body muscles, and indeed nature comes through and provides this for us with no trouble at all. While we dream, there is a shunt or cut-off that comes into operation, preventing the excitement of the dream from reaching the muscles of the body itself.

Most of us have experienced the sensation of this cut-off in operation. Almost everybody I have ever talked to has had the experience of a dream in which they are trying to move (usually trying to run or shout) but are unable to do so. No matter how hard they try, they cannot get their legs to move or get out that scream for help. In this particular dreaming state, we are almost at an awake level. It is close enough to being awake that we are consciously aware of the fact that the dreaming shunt is in operation and that we are not able to actually move our bodies. It's as though we are too close to being awake for the dream to occur in the normal way—and because we are so close to being awake, we realize that we cannot move. Once we waken just a little bit more, the cut-off to our muscles is released and we can move normally.

The brain waves during R.E.M. sleep can show vigorous activity. Sometimes they are even more active than during a period of intense waking concentration. R.E.M. sleep is sometimes called "paradoxic sleep" because your brain is so busy that it seems a miracle that you can remain asleep and that your sleep can be so restful.

Three Basic Modes Of Existence

The state of dreaming sleep differs so completely from Stage IV sleep that some biologists postulate that there are three basic biologic modes of existence. We usually think that there are only two—awake or asleep. Yet because sleep is composed of two such very different types of activity, biologists are beginning to speak of three ways—being awake, being in Stage IV sleep or being in dreaming sleep. Stages II and III of sleep, although distinct, seem to be interim preparatory phases. Interestingly, these same three basic modes are described in ancient Hindu writings, where it was implied that the dreaming state is the stage closest to reality—and it could be that we live to dream.

We Dream To Live

Dreaming sleep is apparently essential for life, so at least we dream to live. If we let an experimental animal sleep but wake him every time he starts to dream, in a period of a month or so he will die. Of course, we have not done this with human beings, but a shorter experiment has been attempted. It is a difficult experiment to do, because often the subjects will quit before the termination of the experiment (which is usually scheduled to last ten days or two weeks). It has been found that those subjects who have been allowed to sleep, but who are deprived of dreaming sleep by the simple expedient of awakening them every time they start to dream, become more irritable after a week or so. They find it difficult to concentrate and may even display neurotic tendencies. They feel as though they have not rested well or haven't slept at all. Their dietary habits change and they may get "a little funny." When the experiment ends and these individuals are allowed to return to a normal pattern of sleep, they tend to spend as much as three times more in dreaming sleep than usual. It is as though the dream mechanism were trying to catch up for lost time to get the brain and body back in balance again.

The Effects of Chemicals And Alcohol

Chemicals that we ingest can interfere with R.E.M. sleep. Most drugs are at least mildly inhibiting, although some have no effect. New awareness of the need for dreaming, both biologically and psychologically, has led conscientious manufacturers of sedatives to seek alternatives to dream supressants. Some of the newer sleeping pills have been specifically designed not to inhibit dreaming sleep.

Alcohol definitely inhibits dreaming. An occasional drinker loses five or ten percent of normal dream time and has a harder time recalling the dreams he has. An alcoholic may suffer from extreme symptoms of dream deprivation. The D.T.'s, or delirium tremens, that come on when an alcoholic stops abruptly after a prolonged period of heavy drinking seem to relate to this. Absence of alcohol suddenly ceases to suppress R.E.M. sleep. The dream mechanism then breaks through with vivid hallucinations while we are awake. These hallucinations, incidentally, very often express symbolically the discomfort and contamination of the internal physical environment of the drinker.

There are very few drugs which stimulate dreaming. One is called reserpine, used in the treatment of high blood pressure. It is produced from Indian black snake root which has been used for centuries as a folk cure for mental illness in the East. If taken for too long a time, its effect may disrupt sleep cycles and cause depression. The only substance I would recommend to facilitate dreaming is Vitamin B-6, called Pyradoxine. It tends to make it easier to recall dreams.

The Dream Pattern

In a normal sleep, undisturbed by experimenters or the neighbor's cat, the usual pattern is for five or six repetitions of the sleep cycle. The first bursts of R.E.M. activity or dreaming which come early in the evening are short—only five to ten minutes long. We may even miss the first dream. Then as the evening progresses, the time spent in Stage IV, or non-dreaming sleep, decreases and the time spent dreaming gets longer. The dreams of the early morning may last up to a half hour or more.

Contrary to popular belief, the flow of time in the dream is exactly the same as when we are awake. If you have a dream that seems to take 15 minutes, and someone is watching you while you are sleeping, they will report that you were dreaming about 15 minutes. If you were dreaming of watching a ping-pong game, your observer would notice that your eyes tended to move from side to side as though you were watching the ball traveling back and forth. You may, of course, have a flashback, just as you can in waking reverie, and see your life in an instant. But if you dream you are running a mile, it will probably take you more than four minutes. It takes the same time awake or asleep.

Why so many people have somehow gotten the idea that every dream occurs in just a second or two, I don't know. This is not the case.

External and Internal Stimuli

You may incorporate the sound of your alarm clock into your last dream, but there is more to dreaming than that brief response. External stimuli, again contrary to popular belief, have very little influence on the nature of your dreams. They seem to be incorporated in the dream only in an attempt to continue the dream process. A passing truck or a snore isn't registered in the dream unless there is a danger that it might awaken us.

Nightmares

Interruptions from within us can break the smooth flow of our cycles. Nightmares are dreams which do not come during R.E.M. sleep. They are not the same as ordinary bad dreams because they force themselves out when the mind is shifting into other parts of the sleep cycle—a time when the ego is not organized to handle dream material. Only intensely felt material has the energy to break in at an unscheduled time, before the dream mechanism can present it in an organized way. The end product is a badly frightening, disorienting nightmare which is hard to interpret. It often takes us a minute or two to reorient ourselves when we awaken from such a dream. Children very often have nightmares. This is probably due to the fact that their nervous system is immature and thus highly emotional material can more easily break through their sleep cycle at the wrong time. In children this is rarely a sign of serious trouble. When it happens, comfort the child until they are reoriented and let them talk about it, if they want to, before they go back to sleep.

Sleepwalking And Talking

Other unusual types of dreams will be discussed in later chapters. The question of walking and talking in sleep is another enigma to the people who are studying sleep and dreaming. These phenomena do not ordinarily occur in dreaming sleep, but very definitely tend to occur during Stage IV sleep. This one little bit of information may be quite significant as time goes on. It seems to indicate the possibility that the mental activity of Stage IV is somehow unique. If you have ever tried to break in on the conversation of a sleep talker, you know they ignore you and keep on talking to someone who isn't there. This response to something so deep within that an outsider can't contact it suggests that dreams may be formed while in Stage IV sleep and then presented to us in R.E.M. sleep. This hasn't been proven, but it is a hypothesis that appeals to me personally and I am presenting it here. It suggests that we make up our dreams first and then show them to ourselves.

We Stage Our Own Dreams

A dream is our own production, of course. We have to write the script and get things rehearsed—and this may be done in non-dreaming sleep. If so, it would explain why events in a dream rarely come as a complete surprise.

The kinds of dreams you have are individually tailored by you. Your level of intelligence, your station in life and the quality of your mental health do not affect the functioning of your dreams, but they do very often determine the type of dreams you may have. Most of us tend to dream in black and white, with only an occasional dream in color. However, those who are artistically trained or are so inclined are more likely to dream in color. Some people think about color more than others. As a result their dreams reflect their way of thinking and occur in color. Most of us pay relatively little attention to the colors around us. We are not interested in them unless it is important, such as a traffic light or something like that. Most of us dream in black and white because it's part of our personality and habits of thought not to notice the variety and moods of colors around us while we are awake. More of us seem to be dreaming in color, however, since the start of color TV.

Studies indicate that most people have dreams resembling black and white silent movies without sound, touch, smell or other sensations—although all sensory modalities can and do appear in dreams from time to time. Your dreams are as personal as your fingerprints. Because they are connected to the unified world of waking experiences, they reveal your attitudes and approach to that world. As Freud says, they are also "the royal road to the unconscious." To make further use of this bountiful resource in a safe and rewarding way, you yourself must learn something about their symbolism and meaning. The purpose of this book is to help you in that study.

In just two decades, sleep research has developed from an almost blank notebook into a mound of reports and observations. We have discovered that sleeping and dreaming are essential to balanced human life and we have developed techniques for exploring the form. Now, over the sea of brain waves we must travel to find the meaning of dreams.

CHAPTER V

Symbols and Their Meanings

There is no single meaning for any one symbol or dream motif. Just like language, they change from person to person because we all mean something slightly different by what we say even though the words are the same. Just like people, symbols change as we study them or as we let them become part of our lives. The net of associations between us grows denser as we come to appreciate their subtle hidden qualities.

This chapter is not meant to be a dictionary of dream symbols. We all use these symbols in different ways depending upon our moods, our interests and our problems at the time they appear in our dreams, as well as our own individual experiences with respect to these symbols in real life.

When we first meet, an introductory tag is helpful. We may be introduced to a new associate with a few tentative connections. This is Mr. Green, a plumber who has three children and who collects stamps. At the beginning Mr. Green is categorized as a stamp collecting, fatherly plumber. Later we may come to know him as that fellow, Herb, who smokes a pipe, yells at his kids and gives us his green stamps. Because our understanding broadens and changes, developing a relationship with another person—and with a symbol—requires attention and rewards us with ever new revelations.

Guidelines To Beginning Dream Interpretation

Guidelines are helpful in the beginning of dream interpretation until we can familiarize ourselves with the personal meaning a symbol has for us. There are standard meanings for symbols that appear frequently, but the dreamer may come up with an original twist or even use a symbol to mean its opposite. We can change the meaning of a word by our tone of voice. By a sarcastic wink, we can make an insult of saying, "He's a nice guy." Dreams change the meaning of symbols in this same way.

This list of symbols is a similar introduction. It is, of course, by no means all of the symbols that appear in your dreams and it's not intended to be a dictionary of a thousand dream symbols. It is merely a list of some of the more common symbols that appear in dreams—the ones that tend to be more powerful and have more of a common thread of meaning running through them. Despite this fact, however, many of them will be presented in an either/or manner, as though they were a two-sided coin (and even at times with many more sides than that), just to give you the understanding that there is no utterly consistent meaning to any particular dream symbol.

Create A Mood

A good way to begin deciphering a dream is to start the way we would with a movie. The first few minutes of the production are usually devoted to creating a mood. The viewer is drawn into the feeling and milieu of the story through scenes of castles or towns or forests, with extras in costume going about their business. As we are led into our dreams, we can try to guess what mood is being created.

Illumination

Begin with the lighting. If the dream is well lit, it is usually a reference to a subject with which we are well acquainted. There is already a lot of light on the subject. When we are in darkness, the dream is probably about some situation that still has us in the dark! If it is at night but the lights are on, we are in a small area of illumination in an otherwise not too well known or understood part of our consciousness. Of course, if you have trouble getting the lights to work, you are obviously talking about an area that you or some other force will not let be illuminated. I remember having several dreams in which I tried to turn on the lights in a room, but they wouldn't work. I felt this meant that something in my basic approach to the subject would not permit me to cast any light on it.

The Setting

Once we have savored the lighting, we must look around at the setting. Are we in a city? In a forest? Are we indoors or outdoors? Are we in the desert? What information does the setting seem to be able to give to us? If a dream is in a place it labels as our own home, it is obviously about an area of consciousness, figuratively speaking, where we live. If the setting is in a bus or a train or a streetcar or some other fairly large commercial vehicle, we are talking about something that involves us as well as a number of other people—some attitude or ideal that we all share in common. If the dream is laid in a foreign country, another state or city, it is probably talking about a state of consciousness that is foreign to or somehow different from our usual way of thinking. Dreams that are placed out of doors are still talking about the world within us but in a more free and open place in our thoughts. Dreams in boats tend to have a somewhat more spiritual connotation, which may be individual or group depending upon the size of the boat and the context of the dream. Of course, if you happen to be a sailor or boating enthusiast, it may refer to work or recreational activities rather than the above. Dreams that take place in airplanes or other mechanical devices that fly generally have to do with flights of ideas, things that you are thinking about doing but as yet have not tried. Sometimes the outcome of these dreams gives you a hint as to whether or not your ideas may be successful if you can get them off the ground. I remember a dream a friend of mine had in which he saw a huge dirigible catch fire and crash in the front yard of his house. The interpretation of this part of the dream indicated that the ideas he had for a project he was contemplating were too grandiose and unwieldy, and if he followed them through he would come to grief.

The Time Frame

The time setting of the dream is also an important factor. It usually refers to a time in your life. For instance, a dream of ancient history or a dream of going through musty volumes looking up old records usually refers to something that went on in very early childhood. A dream of giants may also be a reference to that stage of life. When we are two years old, there really are giants walking on the earth. Dreams that are laid "in the house we grew up in" very often refer to attitudes and ideas that we picked up at that time from the people in that setting. Consequently, a dream of a relative's house at that same time in our lives would have something to do with attitudes or ideas that we picked up from Aunt Mary or Grandmother or whoever it might be.

A costume piece may represent attitudes and ideas handed down to us by heredity or tradition, particularly if the costumes are those of the country of our descent—although the period and the country indicated by the costumes may merely symbolize an attitude within ourselves that is somehow similar to those attitudes of that time and place.

Consider The Surroundings

Many people find themselves in a forest in dreams, which could be an indication of confusion or being lost and unable to find a way home if this is what seems to be going on in the dream. It may be a suggestion that we can't see the forest for the trees, or vice versa. Or it may merely be that we somehow need to get back to nature more in our approach to things. Forests or growths of dense underbrush can have a sexual implication involving the genitalia. The old English word "vagina" means a copse of woods. A virgin forest is an untapped resource, but woods can also be urging us to return to a more natural life. Different species of trees each have a particular significance which has come down to us from the druids. A dream that really highlights the species of tree should suggest to a serious dream student that he look up the meaning of that particular tree in a dictionary, encyclopedia or an anthology of myths. If one of these meanings rings a bell, try it on for size and see if it fits in with the other pieces in the dream.

The terrain can also be quite important. A hill or mountain that we are climbing in a dream almost invariably symbolizes an aspiration that we are struggling towards. If it is a mountain, it may be more spiritual in nature and, of course, certainly more of an effort than just a hill. If we are in a very muddy or swampy terrain, it usually symbolizes something that we are mired down in, either socially or emotionally. Mud being thrown at us, or vice versa, almost always has to do with "mud slinging." Common figures of speech are often the simplest messages in dreams. Coming down a hill may symbolize that "it's all down hill." Farms on the plain are areas in our life that are productive and nourishing to us day by day.

A dream that is set on a battlefield or contains a battle or a struggle usually concerns a conflict or struggle within us. Most of the battles that we fight with others never get to the nose punching stage. We usually work them out within ourselves as we try to come to terms with some general principle or private opinion we have that our partner doesn't.

The Weather Conditions

The weather in a dream is another source of important general consideration. If the weather is stormy, the dream is trying to indicate that things are stormy within us. The storm is usually an emotional one. The wind and the rain and the lightning and the thunder usually indicate various aspects of our emotional upheaval. Lightning, when it is highlighted in a dream, very often indicates a bolt of inspiration and illumination that might be quite traumatic. A dramatic change in our attitudes could come as a "bolt out of the blue."

Rain can indicate a depressing atmosphere, but it is more often a cleansing and refreshing, replenishing symbol in a dream. Rain releases a nourishment that all things need for growing. A rainbow is a promise of things to come. In some dreams it might be a suggestion that we are kidding ourselves about a mythical pot of gold. In the Bible, the rainbow was a symbol of God's promise that he would never again destroy mankind by water. It usually comes after the storm and indicates better days to come. I would certainly feel reassured by a dream of a rainbow.

Water

Water has no color and no shape. It takes the form of its container and the color of its contents. As a result, its symbolic meaning is hard to define. Bodies of water very often have a spiritual connotation. A journey over water is more often symbolic of a spiritual undertaking. Something deep in a body of water may symbolize something deep in the subconscious. Dirty water may be associated with poor health. Water is one symbol that very much takes its meaning from the context in which it appears.

Snow

Snow that is all over the ground can indicate a situation in which things are frozen, in a dormancy that occurs during winter and precedes spring. Snow may have to do with depression as rain does or it may indicate that our assets and abilities lie within us in suspended animation. A snow storm could be a letting out of cold anger.

Fire

The main symbol for anger in a dream is fire. It almost invariably has to do with our anger. The simplest way to remember this is to leave the "f" off and it becomes "ire." Also, where there is smoke there is fire, even if the anger is smoldering underneath. Sometimes "smoke gets in our eyes" and blinds us to what is behind the smoke screen. In some unusual dreams, fire can represent a cleansing or a purifying process that gets rid of our anger and other unwanted attitudes.

The House We Live In

Dreams which are set in our homes, even if they don't look like our houses, tell us about where we live now. We live right here in our bodies. Our minds and spirits reside there and our homes are our most familiar self-construction. Very often the first floor of the home is a dream about our physical body, the second floor is a dream about our mental activities, and the third floor of the home is a dream about our spiritual activities. Dreams set in the basement sometimes have to do with subconscious activities or at other times base "instincts and activities in our consciousness." In this day and age of so many single-story and split-level homes and apartments, this three-story symbolization is not as often used as it has been in times past.

When the front yard or porch of the home is highlighted, it usually refers to things we are showing to the world. Back yard scenes are that area of our life that may be behind the scenes.

The interior of the house and its furnishings are, of course, highly significant. I recall a dream in which an open hallway seemed to suggest that the dreamer was concerned about not being a virgin.

The color of the walls and furnishings may be significant, as well as whether the area is illuminated or not. The various rooms are important. Dreams in the kitchen may have to do with what you are "cooking up" for people. Work areas probably relate to the work you are doing with yourself. Hidden or empty rooms symbolize un-utilized areas of consciousness and potential that we have. Bedrooms very often have to do with sexual themes. Bathrooms usually have to do with cleansing and getting rid of wastes at a mental as well as physical level. If you are asleep in a dream it usually has to do with something you are not aware of.

Radios relate to how you are getting the message and TV's with how you are getting the picture, most likely at the mental level. Telephones have to do with your communicating in the situation the dream is about.

Tables symbolize a common level of consciousness where you and others can work or learn together. The refrigerator and its contents have to do with what is within yourself. Items in the refrigerator that go bad may refer to things you are keeping inside that may be going sour.

Bureaus and chests also have to do with stored items that may not be so emotional or transient as the items in the refrigerator.

Silverware, tableware and other household items tend to relate to what you are doing with them. Flowers may represent lovely thoughts that you want to keep for awhile.

A gun could be a phallic symbol but it also indicates how a person can force their will and/or understanding on another. Being shot may signify a sudden realization or understanding that will change you.

Other Buildings

Dreams in church almost always concern our spiritual attitudes, values or progress. Stores are where we shop for new material, new ideas, new knowledge—but they can also be confusing or tempting. Hotels and motels are usually temporary states of consciousness and attitudes that are being symbolized. If we dream about being in someone else's house, we are being told about our attitude toward them or perhaps the attitudes we get from them. When we are in a large building, the height of the building may have specific meaning for us. I remember one patient who suffered from a manic depressive psychosis. He had a dream of standing on top of a skyscraper. From there he could see far and wide. He then jumped into a lake at its base and had to struggle up through the water to the surface where he found a life preserver. The dream was symbolizing his highs and lows. The life preserver seemed to indicate his medication.

Methods of Transportation

Often dreams are set in automobiles or other motorized vehicles. These dreams are usually about some aspect of our progress through life and the mental powers we use for wheeling and dealing. At other times the vehicle, particularly if it is our own personal car, can symbolize our physical body that we use to get ourselves about in the world. Sometimes it may symbolize our financial or social standing by the way we tend to use our automobiles at the present time. For instance, I remember having a dream in which I traded in my Mustang for another Mustang that was apparently just as good as the car I had labeled "The Boss." At that time in my life I was considering a job offer. The dream was telling me that the new job would be just about as good as the old one, but I could no longer be my own boss. On another occasion, I had a dream in which I was being offered a rich golden brown Cadillac but I was reluctant to pay the price for it. I had this dream at a time in my life when I was making changes in my private practice arrangements. I was reluctant to spend the money that this was going to cost me. The dream was telling me, of course, that I would get into the "Cadillac trade" if I did.

When the dream has to do with a particular mechanical part of the automobile, it may have to do with a particular part of our body. For instance, the air pressure in the tires may be symbolizing our blood pressure. Something wrong with the ignition or battery may indicate a lack of energy, particularly nervous energy, on our part or it may indicate that we merely have our mental wires crossed.

Taxis carry us to our destinations. but we have to pay a fare. Trucks are work vehicles and usually symbolize some aspect of our work. A particular type of truck may indicate a particular aspect of our work. I remember having a dream in which I was driving a dump truck. It had so much dirt in it I could not park it because it kept slipping the brakes. I was trying to park in a nightclub parking lot. The dream indicated that my work load at that time was so heavy that I was not able to really leave it and attend to leisure and pleasure activities.

An interesting example of the use of a bus in a dream to indicate a work load was told to me by a woman friend of mine. She had to take care of her husband and several children, her mother and father-in-law and a brother-in-law and his wife, all in the same house. She asked me one day, "Why is it that I often dream of driving a double-decker bus?" It seemed to me that the symbol of the double-decker bus very graphically symbolized the work load that she had to carry that was obviously double that of the usual housewife.

A train has to follow the track and usually indicates that somehow or other you are "on the track." This may be enhancing your journey or limiting it, depending upon the circumstances. The same is true of streetcars, but they are more local states of consciousness rather than broader ones. A bicycle, on the other hand, can go almost anywhere, but it almost always symbolizes how we are maintaining our balance in our journey through life.

We have already mentioned flying machines. Flying under your own power without a contrivance, that is, levitating, is another aspect of dreams that can be very exciting. It often signifies ideals that have no foundation, a sort of holding yourself up by your own boot-straps, and very often constitutes a warning dream. A young woman I was working with was deluding herself about her relationship with her boyfriend who admittedly did not love her. She dreamed that she and he were floating three feet off the ground and playing a game with each other. The dream indicated that her relationship with the boyfriend had no real foundation and they soon separated. In addition, levitating can indicate levels of sexual excitement. I remember a very amusing short story I once read in which the hero learned how to levitate. Once he got himself up into the air and was flying around the resort where he was staying, he discovered he could not come back down. He was stuck up there for almost a day until finally he saw his very wise girlfriend come out and kiss a fellow who was rivaling him for her affections. At that point he floated back down to earth.

Activities

The activities in which we are engaged are very significant. Some activities are straightforward and easy to understand—struggling up a hill, running away from a fear, pointing the finger, fighting with somebody, clawing at something, eating, etc. When a dream has us struggling with some force or opponent, it is telling us about a struggle within ourselves. A dream of running is probably about attitudes or ideas that the dreamer is running towards or, more often, away from. If we are swimming, perhaps we have "taken the plunge" or we are "in the swim of things" or we are getting along "swimmingly." But if the dream is of drowning or being overwhelmed by the water, something is probably overwhelming us. I remember a dream I heard several years ago from a man who lived on an island in the river. This poor fellow was all alone and had a tremendous work schedule of 16 to 18 hours a day. He repeatedly dreamed that the river was rising up over the island and causing all kinds of trouble. In this case, the rising river represented his fear of being overwhelmed by feelings of inadequacy due to the incredible work schedule that he was maintaining. He managed to keep his head above the water and things did come out all right.

When we play games in a dream, our dreamer is saying figuratively that we are playing a game when perhaps we should be more serious or more honest. Sometimes, of course, we take ourselves too seriously. If we are all tied up in a dream, the meaning is pretty obvious. Eating in dreams indicates taking in nourishment, more often for the mind than for the body. An example of how eating symbolizes food for thought is the dream that a friend of mine had before taking a course in spiritual development. In the dream, she was holding the manuscript we were to study. One of the characters in the dream came up to her and said, "That's just the menu."

I remember another dream in which I was told that for dinner we were going to have back meat. I happened to be in a situation in which there was a good deal of "backbiting" going on.

Dreams of being chased indicate that we are afraid that something, usually within us, may be catching up with us. If we have been trying to fool ourselves, it may be a time for a reckoning. Dreams of falling may help bring us down to earth. Sometimes "pride goeth before a fall." When we are afraid of falling or walking along the edge of a cliff or unsure of our footing, it usually indicates a situation in which our basic understanding is uncertain and may lead to disaster. It is not true that if you fall and hit the ground in your dream you will die. We can dream of dying and survive quite nicely. Dreams where you are lost or can't get to where you are going are talking about situations within you or your life where there is some trouble in reaching your objective.

Dreams of being at a wedding are about forming a union. Parts of our personality may be joining together or we may be entering into a partnership with someone else.

The Cast Of Characters

All the characters in a dream should first be looked at as representing parts of ourselves. If a character plays a part which is not our waking occupation, it may be particularly significant. A doctor most often symbolizes our own healing forces—and what he says and does in the dream might be quite significant with respect to how we are mobilizing, utilizing or paying attention to this aspect of ourselves. Policemen, attorneys and judges all have to do with the law—but usually the laws that are being talked about in our dreams are the laws of nature rather than those made by man. Consequently, a policeman may indicate that we are breaking one of the laws of nature by improper diet, not getting enough sleep or being too cruel to our children. Midgets in a dream may represent facets of ourself that are stunted in growth. Deviations from the norm are parts of the self that aren't quite right. Our babies in a dream indicate growing young projects. If they are newborn, they often represent the birth of an idea or an endeavor on our part. The condition of the baby at birth may be highly significant as to whether or not this idea or endeavor is well-formed. If the child is a few years old, it may refer to an endeavor that has been growing for awhile. Brothers and sisters in the dream, if they are seen clearly, will probably represent attitudes and views concerning these specific people or attitudes that these specific people have towards us. If they are rather indistinct or just mentioned in the dream without being seen, they probably represent your brother and sister in the general sense of the term—your fellowman, male or female. In the same vein, faceless, indistinct individuals also usually represent your fellowman in the general sense. They may, however, represent a part of yourself with which you are as yet unfamiliar.

A dream about a mailman or a telephone man or a letter or a telephone is almost always a dream referring to a communication in one aspect or another. Mailmen bring the message, telephone men establish lines of communication and operators can help make the connection. A fireman represents that facet of self which puts out the fire of ire. A person of low morals, either a known acquaintance or a standardized version, is usually calling attention to the same tendency within self, perhaps as a warning. We recognize the faults of others because we first see them in ourselves. A prostitute may indicate a situation where we are selling ourselves or a situation where we know we can be more capable or honest. Perhaps it indicates that we are using our sexuality in a more material form than we approve of. Ticket sellers, tax collectors and bank tellers are facets of self and life commenting on our ability to pay our own way and keep our accounts straight.

Sometimes we will see a new person in a dream who has no special occupation and they appear very clearly to us. We are then surprised, pleasantly or otherwise, to meet this person in real life a day or so later. Very often the dream will somehow prepare us for the interaction with them—be it positive or negative.

The people we know best—our friends, our family, the people we work with—are most often seen in dreams. When this happens, it is very hard not to immediately assume that the dream is telling us something about that well-known person—and this may indeed be the case. However, before jumping to this kind of interpretation, it is always wisest to first consider this familiar face and figure as symbolizing an aspect of ourselves. The friend or family member in our dream is more often symbolizing something about our attitudes and views towards them or what they represent to us rather than the individuals themselves. In the dream we may exaggerate some negative aspect of this friend's character because that is the way we tend to see them or think of them too often. The dream may be trying to show us how this attitude may lead to difficulties in the relationship. Often, the well-known character in a dream is merely trying to tell us something about the current dream theme. Dreaming about these people is a reminder to look at the part of ourselves that they reflect and examine their meaning for us from different points of view and contexts. Even in waking life, the characters with whom we are most intensely involved mirror some aspect of ourselves. If we ignore this in a dream, we may be missing a deeper, more important meaning of that particular dream.

Characters who are dead are a special case—and this includes ourselves. If we dream that we are dead or dying, we are probably referring to an aspect of our personality which has been put to rest—or perhaps should be. It is not uncommon to dream of being killed, and it doesn't mean that you are finished. Usually the dream is suggesting that some part of you is being terminated, perhaps to pass on to a higher level of development. The same holds true of someone else's dying or being killed in a dream. Every so often a patient of mine will come in with a dream in which they are in a funeral home and the corpse suddenly sits up and starts talking. This usually means that an aspect of the dreamer symbolized by the dead person, which the dreamer had thought was put to rest, is showing signs of reanimation. Turn about, people often come to me disturbed by a dream of having killed someone. These dreams are warning that there is some attitude that they have towards their victim in the dream which should be eliminated before it harms the relationship and perhaps changes it irrevocably. Death in a dream almost always symbolizes a change, because that's what death really is. When you die, for real, you change from one state of being into another.

Another commonly occurring dream symbol is a person who has already died. It may be a parent or a loved one who has died anywhere from a few days to many years before the dream occurs. In this type of dream, the dreamer is most often talking about the attitudes and aspects of himself that relate to the dead individual that have not as yet been entirely resolved by the death. These dreams can give us significant opportunities to work through whatever residual feelings we may have concerning the dead individual, be they positive or negative. Occasionally a dream concerning a dead loved one can be so vivid and so meaningful that it is very hard to accept it as anything other than some direct communication with the departed soul.

School Days

The school dream is another interesting category of symbols that commonly occurs. I think almost everybody has had one of those dreams where you find yourself at school and either you don't have the book or you are not prepared for the exam or you can't find the classroom. These dreams are usually a commentary on the progress of the learning that you need to acquire in your situation in life at the time you have the dream. Consequently, the school in the dream usually symbolizes the "school of life." The type of the school may indicate the particular area in your life where you are trying to learn something. An interesting variation of the school dream that I have run across a number of times occurs in the practiced dreamer who is highly motivated in an on-going learning process. Occasionally these people will dream of being in school where they are actually being taught, in a fairly straightforward manner, some of the concepts they are struggling to learn at the time.

Animals

Animals frequently appear in dreams and usually represent some aspect of our character or personality that can be best symbolized by an animal. Sometimes we are stubborn mules, greedy pigs, wily foxes or just a snake in the grass. On the other hand, animals can symbolize fairly specific aspects of ourselves that are higher in nature. Some of these symbols might be the eagle, the hawk, the snake, the spider, the lion, the tiger, etc. Before getting on to these types of symbols, it might be wise to talk about the chicken so as to give you a good idea of the variability and individuality of any symbol in a dream. The chicken, as a symbol, is an example of the wide range of associations that one animal can have for different people. The participants of a seminar on dreams suggested a catalogue of meanings. Chickens get eaten. They have a pecking order and an awareness of class structure. They scratch in the dirt for bugs. They can be fowl or just another chicken joke. They have a high metabolism and a finely structured body that will allow them to fly if their wings are not clipped. There are brooding hens, proud roosters and peeps. They lay eggs and come home to roost. They can remind us that we are feeling henpecked or just plain "chicken."

Doves are birds of peace and can be a call for peace in a conflict that provoked the dream. Bluebirds wake the thought of happiness. A young woman, who had enjoyed her first sexual experience in secret, dreamed that a bluebird flew out of her eye. To her this meant that her happiness had occurred "out of sight." Robins are harbingers of new beginnings. The peacock, because of its strutting and striding, is usually associated with a show of pride and pomp. Vultures and buzzards may represent tendencies to scavenge. Because these birds are indiscriminate eaters, they are sometimes a warning of dietary indiscretions. An owl usually symbolizes wisdom—or perhaps just looking wise because you don't say much. Owls are also very efficient nighttime predators. An eagle is a fairly specific symbol for the way your heart is flying. The movie title, *The Heart Is A Lonely Hunter,* somehow tunes into this concept. You see, your heart has a great deal more to do with your behavior in areas other than just that of romantic love. It isn't by accident that the eagle is one of the four dramatic symbols in the book of Revelation. The other three symbols are the bull, the man and the lion. The bull symbolizes your basic animal energies that are in part highly sexual in nature. The man, in his various aspects, symbolizes how you utilize these natures in your dealings with your fellowmen. The lion symbolizes how your pride further influences the way you deal with these energies in your daily interactions. The eagle symbolizes these natures turning into a more loving thing, rising above pride and circumstance—but, like the eagle, at times they can become predatory.

Going from an eagle to a hawk is a bigger change than the similarity of the birds might indicate. The hawk is usually symbolizing some of the very highest aspects of your nature and your communication with your Creator. This is why the hawk has a very high place in the symbology that is expressed in much of the Egyptian religious writings.

Sometimes the significance of an animal depends upon whether it is wild or tame. Its domesticity is a clue about how our animal natures are manifesting themselves. A horse, for instance, has many different meanings depending on whether it is a wild horse or one that we can ride. If we can ride and guide it, it certainly indicates that we are in control of this aspect of our animal selves. In either case, the horse in a dream represents a real strength. Another meaning associated with a horse, or particularly a horse and rider, goes back to olden times and has to do with receiving a message or having information come. An elephant indicates great strength, patience and probably long memory. Lions are symbols of ego characteristics and particularly pride. We can be lion-hearted, kingly or bad tempered bellowers. A lion in a dream almost always indicates how our pride is working for or against us. But again, as with most animal symbols, should the lion be either in positive or negative context, it fundamentally indicates a great strength of ours that we need to be able to utilize properly.

A monkey often indicates frivolity, mischief, "making a monkey out of yourself." A stiff-necked giraffe may signify a distortion because of the wide separation between your head and your heart. On the other hand, giraffes are able to see further than most other animals. The lion is the king, but the tiger is the emperor. He is a truly royal beast and his appearance in the dream very often is some sort of comment on the peak of our animal integration. A bear can symbolize a growling bearish anger and resentment. It may have to do with being "over-bearing." But he can also represent formidable tenacious qualities in yourself that could be quite helpful. A bull may symbolize being bull-headed, bullish in nature, quick to anger or quick to sexual excitement, as well as the indications mentioned previously. It is also an ancient symbol of fertility and, of course, to a businessman it may represent a time of increased prosperity.

Cows usually represent some productive aspect of yourself that is nurturing in nature, although you may be as lazy as a cow or as fat as a cow. Pigs have a reputation for being slovenly and greedy. They very often indicate being "pig-headed" about some issue. The significance of the buffalo usually comes from the slang use of the term "to be buffaloed." Crocodiles and alligators are known for their ugly mouths, cruel teeth, dangerous tails and predatory natures. Sometimes they are associated with vicious speech, the aftermath of which may be destructive. The crocodile is an ancient symbol for evil and can sometimes have to do with "crocodile tears." Very often fearsome fishes or beasts that are under the water symbolize subconscious aspects of ourselves that we fear. Turtles, on the other hand, usually represent strength, longevity and patience. The frog is another ancient symbol for evil and may have a bad connotation in the dream.

The snake in a dream is a commonly seen symbol and usually indicates some aspect of a temptation. Those dreams in which we are crossing an area that is crawling with snakes usually indicate an area of our mind that is crawling with thoughts of temptation, usually negative in nature, that may create problems for us if we succumb to them. The snake is also an ancient symbol for wisdom that results from the integration of our lower natures into a higher accomplishment. It is remarkable how worldwide this particular symbol is—from the feathered serpent of ancient Maya to the winged staff of Hermes which is now the caduceus of the medical profession. These are two symbols from two sides of the world, both indicating the ability to integrate your lower natures in such a way as to achieve a higher, more spiritual consciousness. As mentioned above, although the snake most often symbolizes some sort of temptation, if in the dream it is seen with its head raised, such as the cobra, it may be shading over more into this ancient symbol of spiritual wisdom and achievement. If you have ever seen a live king cobra in action, you would begin to get the feel of this symbolic aspect of the snake.

Dogs in dreams usually represent loyalty and trust. This comes from the concept of a dog being man's best friend—"faithful Old Dog Tray." In a dream they very often symbolize how we are doing in our commitments to other people—just how faithful we are or are not being, and other various aspects of the trust other people have placed in us. Cats very often symbolize being "catty" in the slang sense of the word. They are, of course, also extremely independent and not given over to making promises or commitments.

A rabbit tends to be a sex symbol. Rabbits are notorious for their ability to have sex and propogate and usually appear in dreams in this context. At the same time, they can also represent our little rabbity, timid side. In this context, the rabbit is the ideal emblem for the *Playboy* magazine. Individuals who get their sexual stimulation and/or satisfaction from magazines such as this very often tend to have rather strong sex drives but at the same time are too timid to become involved in these areas in real life. Mice represent curiosity or irritations in life of a somewhat minor nature but which might become rather destructive. Rats, on the other hand, tend to have deeper significance as a dream symbol. Rats carry disease from one place to another. If you split that into "dis-ease" (uneasiness), it can often mean that rats seen in a dream are associated with gossip (which is "dis-ease" that people carry from one place to another). If a rat appears in a dream it is a symbol to be looked at fairly closely.

Bugs, beetles and vermin represent annoyances and aggravations that are flitting about in your mind. We may feel that we are being bugged in one sense or another. Bees have to do with the stings of life and yet can be very cooperative and industrious in making money. Worms may symbolize what might happen if you open that "can of worms." Lice and other vermin represent uncleanness of body, mind or spirit. When you are "lousy" you are not very good in your habits of personal grooming or perhaps thinking.

A spider is another very potent symbol. Spiders weave webs that entangle and entrap us and usually represent an influence or a person that is engaged in this activity about us. These dreams are very often warnings that we may be getting caught in a web of intrigue or indiscretion. I remember a patient of mine who was planning to marry. She had a vivid dream involving a large spider with purple knee-bands. Despite the warning in the dream she married anyhow and soon found herself entangled in an incredible web of intrigue in her husband's family that eventually resulted in her husband's suicide.

Fish are another very important symbol. They usually symbolize spiritual food if the fish in the dream is to be eaten. If the fish is not being eaten but is seen as swimming about, it is again usually a comment on some aspect of our spiritual development. This is an archetypal symbol and it is not by accident that it was utilized by both the early Christians and Jews for representing the spiritual side of their religions. Dangerous and predatory fish such as sharks and piranha represent distortions of these spiritual values that can cause great harm. You can understand what these symbolize by thinking of the viciousness of individuals who are trying to prove themselves spiritually better than someone else or trying to defend their spiritual beliefs for whatever reason. A whale brings a big lesson or a "whale of a tale" or perhaps something incredibly deep and momentous in our personalities. This is how the whale Moby Dick was used as a symbol in the novel.

You may start working with your dreams by using these common interpretations, but eventually you will begin to develop your own symbol list of meanings. As there are frequent references in our dream journals of symbols that do not fit these suggested meanings, we can begin to see what those symbols share and start to catalogue our own dream dictionaries. Each dreamer uses his own personal language which can only be deciphered with time and attention—and in the final analysis can only be deciphered by himself.

CHAPTER VI

Symbols and Their Meanings— A Deeper Look

Legend tells us that when Genghis Khan swept down to conquer China and unabashedly massacred those who resisted, one brave Chinese king was captured alive. The nobility and audacity of the conquered ruler pleased the Khan, and he engaged his captive as tutor for his grandson. When that grandson became ruler of the Mongol Empire, the old Chinese tutor was secretly the final victor. He had instilled the young Mongol with the basic values of Chinese culture, and the young man, Kublai Khan, became one of China's most enlightened rulers.

When rational science swept across Europe to conquer Western thought, it could not kill off the most powerful ideals which influenced the minds of all people. Instead, it captured those ideals and pressed them into service to amuse and tutor children with fairy stories, card games, holidays and art. While science has been building our civilization, this suppressed corps of ideals has tutored us all in the underlying values which ultimately shape our culture. While our science has taught us to industrialize and mechanize the forms of our culture, the suppressed ideals have been content to show us a model for our own humanization.

The ideals which have endured do so because they have always been powerful rulers in their own right. The wise old woman, the hero, the Merlin magician, the pure unicorn, the dragon, etc., all represent realms of deep human experience. Those realms could be rationally suppressed, but they could not be destroyed without sterilizing the whole terrain of feeling, cutting the mind off from its support and sustenance. Fortunately the suppressed ideals have survived, and they have kept alive the ancient understanding of which they are the guardians.

When the Mongol lords ruled China, most of them didn't attempt to learn the complex and subtle language of their conquered subjects.

This allowed Chinese writers great freedom if they were discreet. Thus the literature of that period is full of open criticism of the Mongols. The messages of our dreams can be critical of our day to day living and candidly reveal the most sacred teachings which we miss until we learn the complex and subtle language of our poetic dreams. It is not the language of everyday prose. It is the language of myth and religion and poetry.

The secret is unity. It is ever before us and all of our systems depend on it. It is so simple that when we hear it spoken by children, we dismiss it lightly and return to our preoccupation with the particular concerns of the moment. The theme which our dreams present, clothed in their multifarious plots, is the unity of all being. We and the universe are one. Do unto others as you would have them do unto you. And yet in the unity there is diversity.

Archetypes

Until our conscious minds have tired of fascination with facts and figures and have recognized the insufficiency of rational science, the ideals wait with enduring patience. Until our conscious minds have evolved to be able to comprehend the fundamental concept which these ideals serve, they remain grey-cloaked mentors, disguising themselves with infinite variety to educate us as they amuse us. Carl Jung recognized these concepts held in the unconscious mind and he called them archetypes. He believed that they were symbols of major experiences shared by the entire human race. The memory of these lessons was inherited by each individual and, because it was shared, served as a means of communicating. If archetypes were only the symbols for past events, they would be like lifeless archaeological relics which derive their significance from a lost culture's ritual. The archetypes which guide our growth are much too vital to be mere relics. The concepts which have been recorded in all mythologies are remembered because they are somehow shared by us all. They are selected as being memorable because they serve as illustrative examples of this unity. That concept is the living basis of all life—and the archetypes are its active ministers.

All symbols depend on this underlying unity. A house in a dream can represent a physical body because in some way house and body are connected. All words and other symbols subtly convey this concept, but archetypal symbols have unity as their primary meaning. They can be recognized by their emphasis on humanness and by the power they exude. When they appear in dreams, they have the feeling of being important even when they are in supporting roles.

The primary archetype is the symbol for man's higher self. When these figures appear in dreams they can be deeply stirring experiences. They are the models for our full development. They can also appear with helpful advice about our relations to other people. An old sea captain, a bishop, a teacher, a wise man, gods and goddesses, or even a disembodied voice may come in a dream to tell us how to raise our children or understand our co-workers. They are symbolized as any wise, experienced, respected guiding figure.

Dominant—Receptive

The next most powerful archetype is seen as a being of the opposite sex from the dreamer. Jung called this other self the *anima* in men and the *animus* in women. It represents that necessary complementary self and it can appear in either a negative or a positive aspect. You see, to be balanced, effective and truly creative human beings, we need both modes—masculine and feminine—dominant and receptive—to be operating in coordination within us. If this is not so, it affects all of our relationships because all human interaction involves these two modes of behavior.

A conversation is the simplest example. The person speaking is dominant; the listener is receptive. This receptivity is somehow feminine and gestative because when the speaker stops, the listener must come forth with a reply and in turn becomes dominant. To be good at this, a person must be able to easily shift back and forth between masculine and feminine or dominate-receptive modes of behavior.

If one forces dominance in a conversation, they only learn what they are saying. If one forces receptivity, they only learn what the other person is saying. In either case, there is no true sharing of viewpoints and it ends in a no-growth situation instead of one that enhances both parties. The same is true of all other types of human interaction.

Because how we are operating in both these modes is so important to our development, our dreams are full of comments about this. Almost all of those dreams in which there is significant male-female interaction are comments about our progress, or lack of it, in this area. If either figure is creating problems, that aspect of ourselves is out of balance both within us and our interactions. As we balance our innerselves, the male and female figures take on more benevolent aspects. Eventually we dream that they are getting along quite well.

Symbol systems like the zodiac, the tarot and numerology are based on other aspects of the archetypal model of humanness. Dream interpreters can profit greatly by studying the language of these occult systems because they were constructed to mirror archetypal man, who appears in the symbology of the myths of all cultures. The zodiac, tarot, numerology and other ancient esoteric teachings are all conscious attempts to express the truth of our progress toward unity with God through their particular symbology.

Parts Of The Body

"The Grand Man of the Universe" is a system that comes out of the zodiac and gives clues to the meaning of many dreams. When parts of the body are highlighted in a dream, the Grand Man concept can be used as a bridge between these physical parts and their mental and spiritual significance in the development of the dreamer. When the parts of the body appear in a dream engaged in a general activity, the primary meaning usually relates to the activity (such as clawing hands, pointing fingers or running feet). When the body part is not engaged in purposeful activity and is passively highlighted in some way (such as being touched, observed, bejeweled, hurt, etc.), it may be utilizing the more esoteric or Grand Man of the universe symbology. Even if one doesn't believe in astrology (and we are not promoting it), this aspect of it is a pervasive archetypical symbology which may appear in our dreams and is therefore important to the student of dreams.

In this system the parts derive their most potent significance from their relation to the whole. Body parts represent stages in the development of human consciousness. Each location in the body is the symbol for the conflict between the positive and negative energies which must be balanced at that stage.

According to the symbolism of the Grand Man of the Universe, the head indicates the *I AM* part of the dreamer and relates to the sign of Aries in astrology. Here one experiences the conflict between centering oneself with genuine awareness against narcissistic ego-tripping. The neck, when highlighted in a dream, has to do with willfulness. Its astrological counterpart is Taurus. A bullnecked personality exemplifies this quality of willfulness. The thyroid gland, which is associated with willfulness, is located in the throat area. The conflict expressed is whether or not the dreamer is being willfully constructive or not. We must all learn to do the will of God. It's no good to be stiffnecked about things.

The hands very often have to do with what we are thinking. Hands are what we use to do things in the world outside ourselves. Thoughts are what we use to do things inside ourselves. Hands express outside what we decide to do inside. The shoulders, arms and hands all correlate with the zodiac sign of Gemini. The twins also symbolize changing thought and are associated at times with the trouble we have making up our minds.

The stomach and breasts are ruled by the sun sign Cancer and relate to giving and receiving. They connotate an awareness of the needs of others as well as our own. They show the conflict between giving out nourishment and taking in. Many stomach disorders such as ulcers arise from a conflict between these two needs. I recall a young lady who was seeing me for, among other things, a weight problem. She dreamt that a bug bit her on the right breast. The dream was suggesting that the solution to her problem lay more in the area of giving out than taking in.

The heart and backbone, which are the domain of Leo, is the area where the conflict between love and the pride of misdirected will is waged. To be small-hearted is to not have the courage to face the issue. The heart relates to feelings as the stomach relates to needs. To be big-hearted is to make others feel good about themselves by giving of ourselves. A spineless individual does not have the foundation in his personality to deal with the issue at hand.

The area of the back by the kidneys (called the "reins" and ruled by Virgo) is related to how we deal in our friendships. The reins are the seat of affection. When dreams highlight this area, they may be pointing out the conflict that arises when our tendency to be open and loving is inhibited by our being too self-centered. Very often backaches arise in this type of situation. It is false pride which builds the ego at the expense of others by saying, "I'm better than he is." A true pride sees that we are all working together and accepts our own attributes and abilities to be used to help the common effort.

The bowels, ruled by Libra, are related to giving and withholding. They are also the area which symbolizes our feeling about how our giving is received and, as a result, oddly enough, have a lot to say about love.

The genitals, ruled astrologically by Scorpio, symbolizes willful desire and the conflicts generated by sexual frustration. The lesson is to begin to learn that pleasure is just another sensation. Then we are no longer so much driven by sexual and other frustrations, and Scorpio's other symbol, the Phoenix, is more applicable to us.

The last four signs of the zodiac are traditionally related to the lower limbs. In this analogy, consciousness moves down from the head to infuse the foundations of the Grand Man and his ability to move. The thighs, ruled by Sagittarius, are the mainspring for independent movement. When the upper legs are highlighted in a dream, it emphasizes our out-going, or on-going nature, either physically or socially. The thighs are also used to form a lap, and the conflict which centers in this area is between being out-going and needing to hold back. Sagittarius is a horse with a man's chest, heart and head—and it symbolizes the balanced control of a rider on a powerful steed.

The knees are the flexible joints in our support and they represent using our material existence to climb to higher philosophical levels. The coordination between support and the flexibility that enables one to climb resolves itself here with prudence and well thought-out actions—learning not to be so over-burdened by our attachment to worldly possessions that our knees can't bend properly.

In our calves and ankles are the muscles which turn our feet from side to side as we direct our path. This area, which is ruled by the sign of Aquarius, has to do with choosing. The conflict is between being inventive and conventional, as if at some level we know the way but have to choose to turn to it.

The feet are the foundations. They represent our understanding of our own nature and the nature of each situation and person we meet. If the feet become mired in material concerns, they are slow to take the steps necessary for growth. But we must have down-to-earth contacts to support our work. They implement our purpose and symbolize the understanding, knowledge and faith necessary to do so.

We strive to develop consciousness through the whole body of the Grand Man within ourselves and to balance the conflicts in our being, willing, thinking, feeling, analyzing , desiring and progressing—eventually developing true faith, understanding and patience. Often when our dreams focus on some part of the body, they are advising us that we need to work at balancing the conflict which that part represents in our development as a unified, whole individual.

The symbolism of these twelve archetypal body areas is supplemented by other body parts which also can be interpreted as reports on our physical, mental or spiritual balance. Hair most often symbolizes thoughts which come out of the head. For instance, the story of Samson is an allegory on concentration. Samson's strength, cut short by Delilah, came from his ability to concentrate on his spiritual ideals. Coloring hair, fixing hair or cutting hair usually represents how we are organizing and changing the appearance of what we are thinking. The eyes, which have been called the windows of the soul, can be highlighted in a dream which is attempting to give us a glimpse directly into the state of our souls. They can also mean the "I" or the ego. If the "I" is blinded, the ego is left fumbling in the dark. Eyes can also represent sight, both inner and outer. How well we are seeing a situation might be the message they try to convey. Very often these ideas may be represented in a dream by our inability to see because our glasses are broken or missing or perhaps "rose colored."

Ears have to do with hearing or with those things to which we are deaf because of our attitudes. They are also symbols for harmony and discord on the more general level.

The nose, which is responsible for warning us of strange odors, is also used to distinguish subtle differences in what we take into our mouths. Therefore, the nose may represent discrimination. However, the discrimination can be false if we are stuck up with our noses in the air.

The mouth and teeth can symbolize our ability to bite and be aggressive, but usually when the mouth, teeth or tongue appear in a dream they are referring more often to what comes out of them, i.e., our speech. Teeth, for some reason, most often figure in this type of interpretation. They are one of the gates of the tongue. I am reminded here of a dream told to me by Hugh Lynn Cayce. A man who came to visit him talked incessantly all evening long. In the course of the conversation he mentioned that he had a repeated dream that his teeth were falling out of his mouth at such a rate they made a huge pile on the floor. He was a person who couldn't shut up, and his dreams were trying to point this out. The teeth in their role as a barrier to the tongue were not working. One unusual interpretation concerning teeth is that if you dream of losing a single tooth it can be predictive of the fact that you are about to lose a friend. Why this is, I do not know, but it is surprising how very often this particular interpretation works out.

When the symbol of body hair appears in a dream, it often refers to sensitivity. The hair on the skin increases our sensitivity to touch. Sometimes, however, if it grows in large quantities in a dream, it may be indicative of more coarse qualities.

Fingers, in and of themselves, don't seem to have much specific meaning in dreams other than the action in which they are engaged—such as beckoning, accusing, pointing, "giving the finger" to someone. Sometimes the conformation of the fingers may have a significant meaning, depending on the way they are shown (such as their being clawlike, slender or sturdy).

Toes very seldom figure as specific symbols in interpreting a dream. They usually have to do with particular points about your understanding—the ground that you stand on, so to speak, in your inner mind. The great toe can be used as a symbol of your ability to balance and propel yourself forward. Feet have to do with the purpose of our life or our real understanding of our existence as individuals.

Blood is a common dream symbol. It is the fluid that energizes all of our body. Consequently, bleeding or loss of blood symbolizes loss of or wasted energy. Menstrual bleeding, however, tends to indicate a cleansing process.

Body Sensations

Next we should consider body sensations such as that of being touched or bitten, burned, lifted up, suffering indigestion, having to go to the toilet, etc. These occur rather infrequently in dreams. When they do, I feel that most often they tend to emphasize that part of the body in which they occur. In other words, if somebody touches you on the left shoulder, the touch itself has meaning in terms of communication or getting in touch with, but the left shoulder also has specific meaning in terms of its being on the receptive side of the body.

As an example of what I'm talking about, I'm reminded of a patient of mine. A young lady who was very seriously ill came in one day and announced that she had had a dream in which she had been bitten in the right loin, or kidney area, by an undetermined animal. She said, "The darn thing bit me right here," and pointed to this particular area of her body. Now this is a rather difficult place for a specific interpretation on the surface, especially since her level of thinking at that time really wasn't quite up to understanding much in the way of interpreting dreams. It's not surprising to find that following this particular dream this young lady began to show a steady and gratifying improvement in her condition. Her illness was characterized by an unusually infantile, selfish attitude. After the dream she began to show a definite and gratifying increase in her awareness of the needs and problems of others and a desire to help them. When you go back into some of the old esoteric kinds of literature, it is indicated that the reins are referred to as "the seat of the affections." When you relate this to the various glands in the body, it fits in with the adrenals. It was as though by her dream this particular patient was indicating that this center or part of herself was being stimulated, activated and reawakened. With this activation, she began to change in her direction and show a substantial improvement.

Sometimes body sensations can be a direct recall at this level of a past event in one's life that is important and perhaps needs some sort of re-evaluation. You know the old story about falling off a horse. It's always wise to get back on the horse again as soon as you can. All of us have physically painful and uncomfortable experiences of one kind or another that for various reasons we can't redo in our minds right at the moment. We tend to forget or avoid thinking about these experiences, then later on find ourselves flinching without understanding why. Dreams will try to bring back these actual physical sensations in order to bring this event to mind for re-evaluation so that it won't give you quite as much trouble.

The most common example of this is the repeated nightmares some people tend to have after a really traumatic event. These dreams, though unpleasant, are actually helping the person run out the fear and pain of the event. I am reminded of a youngster I saw who had experienced painful and terrifying second degree burns over her whole body. After the event she had repeated nightmares about fire. When it was explained to her and the family what these dreams were trying to accomplish, she did much better and began to lose her waking terror of fire.

Another use for somatic sensations that occurs with me and incidentally, brings up a question as to the purpose of dreaming, is that during the day I have the ability of taking a cat nap and saying to myself that I'll wake up in 20 minutes (or half an hour, or some other specified time). At the end of 20 minutes, I will have a sudden quick dream, such as being slapped across the face with a wet towel or hearing an explosion, that startles me awake. I'm convinced that the purpose of these dreams is to awaken me.

Articles of Clothing

Next we should consider some of the meanings placed on articles of clothing in dreams. It's a natural progress to go from parts of the body to the types of covering or clothing you use for them and their significance in dreams.

The clothing with which we cover our bodies in dreams is symbolic of how we dress or show our attitudes and views. The color of the clothing very often has considerable significance, as does the quality and appropriateness of the garments. Being undressed, naked or partially dressed indicates being unprotected at a general level or being exposed in a social way.

When you think about clothing in the real world, it's very often used as a way of indicating what our occupation is. Professional men must dress accordingly or people won't put much stock in them. We recognize policemen, nurses, flyers, soldiers, repairmen and many other occupations by their uniforms. Almost every occupation has its specific dress code which is used in labeling a person at first meeting. Even non-conformists these days seem to conform to specific non-conformist ways of dressing. Consequently, in a dream, clothing can serve this very same function—to identify figures as to occupation and attitudes. Changing your clothing in a dream very often indicates a change in occupation or a change in attitude in your approach to a particular situation.

Hats very often symbolize the way we dress our egos. There is the cloak of pride. There is the bodice of sorrow. There is the belt that is perhaps a bit too tight. There are the boots of power that sometimes walk on people, and there are the socks that protect but sometimes cover our understanding. You can go on this way with many of the different articles of clothing that we commonly wear.

At times, articles of clothing may symbolize what is directly underneath them. For instance, a necktie may indicate specific attitudes and "ties" according to its color and associations, but it can also symbolize something going on inside the chest or throat. The same is true for necklaces, chokers, pins, etc.

Gloves very often represent how we cover and protect our thoughts and intentions. Incidentally, gloves are often shown as being either black or white in dreams. By this, they may also represent the nature of the thoughts themselves.

Colors

The color spectrum is another universal archetypal symbol for wholeness. The white light breaks down into a rainbow, and each color has a range of meanings depending on its clarity and intensity. A dream in color, especially for those who usually dream in black and white, is often rich in spiritual or emotional meaning. Because it is more colorful, it attracts attention and prompts analysis. As specific color may be highlighted by the context of the dream and traditional color symbolism can be a helpful aid in extracting its meaning.

Sometimes a color will appear in a black and white dream. In this case, the color has a very specific meaning. These meanings are not too hard to understand. Many of them can be obtained from common figures of speech—such as being red with anger, green with envy, feeling blue or having a purple passion. These figures of speech do not occur by accident. They relate to the specific symbolic meaning of the color mentioned.

The quality of a color is quite important in its interpretation. If it's a good clear strong color, then generally the interpretation is on the positive side. Where the color is dark and murky or dirty, the connotation is usually negative. If the shade is pastel, it's a more delicate kind of interpretation that you make.

White is all the colors mixed together. It is the color of completeness, of purity, of innocence and of cleanliness. The color white usually has a very positive, good connotation associated with it. In some cultures it is the color of death because death in these cultures is seen as a new beginning.

The color black, on the other hand, is generally the color of the unknown and of the fear associated with the unknown. Things that are in darkness in a dream are literally in darkness. We don't know them or understand them. And things that have a black color about them highlighted in a dream have to do with something unknown.

Red is the first of the primary colors and usually indicates force, vigor and energy. Its interpretation depends on the shade and, as with all colors, the relationship with other colors and symbols in the dream. Dark red indicates anger and is the nervous turmoil that goes with it. Scarlet often has to do with ego. Pink or coral is the color of immaturity. Red is sometimes the color of war and sacrifice. A rich rose is the color of love.

Different shades make all the difference, as is shown by comparison of two dreams in which different reds were highlighted. A man I had never met before asked me about a dream. He said that in his dream somebody was getting married and everything was red—the clothes, the carpet, the walls, the ceiling—everything. I told the fellow that it sounded as though the dream was talking about a union being formed in anger. After a moment's pause he admitted that just might be so. Another dream was set in a house where everything was in a beautiful baby pink. The interpretation had to do with the immaturity of the dreamer and again fit almost exactly. You'll be surprised how precise these colors can be. It's rather tricky when you're working with someone else's dreams because it's hard for them to convey the actual tone and quality of the color and its feeling. But in recalling your own dreams, it's tremendously helpful.

Orange is the color of friendship, or sometimes the color of desire. It is a vital, good color, generally indicating thoughtfulness and consideration of others. Orange can also signify glory, virtue and the fruits of the earth. In the Orient, orange is the color worn by those who renounce all desire.

Yellow is the color of thought. It stimulates the mind. Some scientific material is printed on yellow paper for this reason. When the material stimulates the base emotions the quality of the yellow is bad and it's called "Yellow Journalism." Golden yellow indicates health and well-being. Yellow when it's tainted with green (not a chartreuse exactly but a dirty yellow-green) very often is predictive of some kind of poor health.

Green is the middle color in the spectrum, so green is the stabilizing color. Pure emerald green, particularly if it has a little blue in it, is the color of healing and good health. As it tends towards blue, it's more healthful and trustworthy. As it tends toward yellow, it is weakened. A lemon green with a lot of yellow in it gets into envy, which may turn deceitful. If it is dirty, it is the color of poor health. You see how the quality of the color is so important in making the interpretation. Green can also symbolize youthfulness and the fertility of nature—like the burgeoning green of the Spring, full of good things that are coming along.

Blue has almost always been the color of the spirit, being the symbol of contemplation or completion, prayer, heaven and so forth. We say in common speech, "He's true blue," and this is one connotation. A pale blue tends to indicate a struggle towards maturity, and a deep blue is a more substantial indication that we are "right on." This color is associated with the higher attainments of the soul. In the Book of Revelation, the throne at the middle of the sea of glass is sapphire. Again, if the color is murky, you are off, and it very often indicates depression. Depression is usually the result of not obtaining your goal for self. When depressed, you definitely don't feel "right on"—and the color, being off, expresses this.

I'm reminded here of a friend of mine who has a tendency towards periodic and very severe depressions. They weren't quite bad enough to seek help, but they gave him a lot of trouble. When they came on, he just sat and did nothing. I remember him talking one day of having a dream in which he was sitting in a car that had stalled in a snow storm. The snow was coming up over the windows and it was blue. It symbolized neatly that when he got depressed, he was frozen or stopped. The color in this case indicated depression, while the snow and the stopped car indicated his frozen inner assets.

Indigo or purple is the color that symbolizes the process in which we begin to mobilize our energy to maintain what we have in the blue. Hence comes the phrase "purple passion" when we carry this to extremes. This color is also associated with royalty because the king's main job is to keep the kingdom stable and prosperous. Purple finally gives way to lavender, which is the color of seeking. It is the highest color in the spectrum—but that is not necessarily indicative of the highest attainments. It is not a color that is well balanced, like a good blue is. It is a color that comes when the achievements get old and we must seek again. The statue of the Winged Victory portrays the goddess Athena posed on her toes with her wings outspread—which is a kind of after-completion. She's already made it; she's won the victory. But like everyone else, once the goal is achieved, she becomes restless and ready to take off for the next one. This is the idea of the color lavender. A seeker, moving ahead, is never content for long. Lavender is desirable in terms of seeking and moving on and trying to strive for new understandings, for the better things that come out of new challenges.

The color brown is a very good color indeed. Many people suspect it of having rather earthy, uncomfortable or unpleasant interpretations. However, a good healthy, rich brown is indicative of proper orientation and functioning at the earth level. Sometimes it has to do with money. Old traditions tell that if you wish to acquire money, you should use a wallet of a good rich brown color. If the brown becomes muddy or dirty, the connotation is just that—of a muddy situation in which the dreamer is less sure and less secure. It may symbolize a confused orientation at the earth level when your footing is a little slippery.

Gold and silver are often seen in dreams. Gold corresponds to the mystical aspects of the sun and silver corresponds to the moon. The color gold is the image of sunlight and hence of divine intelligence. It has the quality of superiority indicative of spiritual richness and it symbolizes the light from God. The color silver, like the moon, symbolizes how we reflect this light in our minds. Silver has to do more with mental activity—quick thinking like quicksilver. Silver is ephemeral and stimulating. Gold is a more solid color and, although it is not quite as quick, it has a healing, stabilizing connotation. We have been talking about the colors gold and silver, and not the substance. This distinction is necessary because very often the substance gold or silver will appear in dreams and usually has to do with riches of the mind and spirit. Almost invariably when you see money, particularly gold, the dream is talking about mental and spiritual worth rather than actual material worth—inner assets, self-worth, rather than material wealth. Don't lose track of the fact that dreams primarily talk about the world inside.

Sounds

Next we would like to talk about sounds. Sounds in dreams seem to fall into a category rather similar to color, but with some differences. During the day most of us are concerned with the meaning of the sounds we hear rather than the specific quality of the tone or the timbre in a person's voice. Consequently, the meanings of a conversation routinely appear in dreams but the sounds themselves are not so often met with. Most people dream, as I said earlier, in black and white. Likewise, if a conversation goes on in a dream you don't usually hear it as such, but you know what is being said. In waking life you are thinking of the meaning of the words going back and forth but usually don't pay attention to the sound of the words themselves.

This is the way it is with most of us from day to day, or from minute to minute in our daily living. We are more concerned with the meaning of events rather than their sensory vehicle.

Just as colors have specific meanings and are particularly significant, smells, tastes and sounds can be used to emphasize the meaning of a particular symbol in a dream—such as hearing the rush of the wind when you're dreaming of the whirlwind of an emotional conflict or a storm.

Songs in dreams crop up every so often and are a lot of fun to work with. Usually the meaning is hidden somewhere in the title of the song or in the words, or it might pertain to the particular association it has when we hear it. Specific tones may have specific meanings in dreams, as do the colors. They are similar to the meanings of the colors, but I've never known anyone who was sufficiently trained musically to pick up this kind of thing. In esoteric symbology they tend to run the musical scale with colors in the same fashion. They are always given this way, with the note "do" corresponding to the red in the spectrum, the note "re" to the orange, and so forth. Whether or not this actually occurs in dreams, I don't know. I've never had a piano tuner for a patient.

Numbers

In a dream, numbers do have a specific meaning for the dreamer. Sometimes it may be something relatively simple, such as something is about to happen in five days—symbolized by seeing five sunflowers. This kind of simple counting may be the most important message for the dreamer at the time.

Numbers, however, have a deeper meaning that is an ancient and archetypal one. Numerology is the study of numbers prior to their use in mathematics. It is a very ancient science. Although not highly regarded today it is very useful in working with numbers when they appear in dreams. In this system, a number of more than one digit is first reduced to a single digit number. This single digit number is then considered to be the main meaning of the more complex number seen in the dream. Then the original single digits are considered to indicate how you arrived at that main meaning.

In reducing a number, you add the digits together. You continue to

Interpreting Your Dreams

do this until it reduces to one single digit. The number 194 in a dream would reduce to 5—1 plus 9 plus 4 is 14. The 14 can be broken down even further—1 plus 4 equals 5. The prime meaning of the original number (194) is taken from this reduced number (5). At the same time, the individual digits in the number should be considered to provide additional meaning to a particular symbol. With the number 194 you would first check the significance of 5. Then you would look up 1, 9 and 4 because they are the means by which you will achieve the 5 as it appears in this dream context.

What follows here is a very brief outline of the meanings of the various numbers according to the principles of the science of numerology. As I have indicated, the study of numbers has been a preoccupation of mankind since earliest history. You will have to familiarize yourself with these basic concepts and think about them. Perhaps you might want to play around with them in various ways, like finding out what the numbers for your birthdate reduce to. After a while you will begin to get a feeling for the meanings of numbers as signposts of various kinds and find that they can be quite helpful in working with your dreams. It is also interesting to note that the progression of numbers from 1 through 12 seems to indicate a progression in the development of an individual, just as seemed to be the case when we were studying the symbolic meanings of the body parts going from the head to the feet.

ONE is unity, is ego, is strength, is the beginning or origin place.

TWO represents the first division, and it can either be strong, if the two parts are working together, or weak, if they are in opposition. The most important thing about the "2" is that you need two elements in order to be truly creative.

THREE is the result of that creation at a mental level. It is the idea or the concept which has the strength of "1" and the weaker sort of "2." It can either be manifested or changed.

FOUR is taking that idea or concept and bringing it into material manifestation. It is the number of the material world where things tend to be four-square.

FIVE is where the individual begins to explore the material world further and thereby develops the ability to change and adapt to the circumstances in the material world. "5" is the number of change—but oddly enough it is the middle number in the single digit spectrum and consequently has a great deal to do with stability as well. Perhaps this is because "the only thing permanent is change." Sometimes "5" is considered to be the Christ number.

SIX is the number of balance between the mental and physical aspects of the individual. It is the number of some power because of the harmony and balance that the individual has been able to achieve both within and without.

SEVEN is the number of spiritual awareness. It is a number signifying the things we learn in our spiritual advancement.

EIGHT is another number of power and weakness. It symbolizes the ability to balance the spiritual knowledge gained at the "7," with material and mental understanding. When these are in balance they represent true power. Sometimes "8" is associated with money.

NINE is the number of completion in which the individual has achieved a balancing and a functioning at all three levels—physical, mental and spiritual. It proceeds on to the "10."

TEN is a new beginning at another level in which the individual is becoming more aware of the meanings behind the universe.

ELEVEN is the number of increased awareness at this level and is sometimes called the number of physical mastery.

TWELVE is the completion of another cycle which indicates the integration of ourselves with the universe as a whole but it goes on to "13."

THIRTEEN is where things once again change and a new awareness is mandated.

TWENTY-TWO is sometimes called the number of mental mastery and certainly involves the ability to make right choices.

THIRTY-THREE is sometimes called the number of spiritual mastery and is a number of significant completion.

In working with numbers in dreams, it is usually best to limit yourself to the numbers 1 through 9, only occasionally employing the higher numbers in special cases.

When zeros appear in a number that you see in a dream, if they are at the end of the number they are generally placed there for emphasis. In other words, 5,000 appearing in a dream would be much more important than if it were just the number 5 because of the emphasis of the zeros. Sometimes when the zero appears in the middle of the number (for instance 207) you may want to treat it as two separate numbers—a 2 and a 7, rather than as a single number 9. The decimal point appearing in a number, such as an item costing $3.95, also suggests that you should treat it as two separate numbers—the 3 and the reduction of 9 and 5 which is 5.

Now to give an example of the significance of numbers in dreams, I recall a dream in which the dreamer was buying a new car for himself for a price of $140. This transaction was the entire dream, so obviously the interpretation depended upon the number 140. The new car in the dream was something that the man wanted, a new way of doing things for himself. But the dream said that he had to pay a price for it and the price was $140. The numbers in this price reduce to 5. To have this new thing for himself he had to change, because 5 is the number of change. The individual digits are also significant. The 1 reminded the dreamer that he had to be more self-assertive, more a forceful unit in and of himself. The 4 indicated that he had to be more organized at a down-to-earth level to be able to accomplish the change he wanted, represented by the new car he was trying to buy. The number in this particular dream clearly indicated to this gentleman the price he should be prepared to pay if he wanted to take on a new way of doing things for himself. The zero indicated he had more work to do with himself before he could come up with the price.

This chapter contains some of the basic archetypal symbols and their meanings. They are deep and require some thought to understand. How is it that they appear with the same meanings in the dreams of children as well as adults?

CHAPTER VII

How To Work With Your Dreams

Most of us wake up in the morning with little or no recall of the dreaming that went on while we were asleep. The alarm goes off and we quickly get involved in the day's activities. Sometimes a few fragments of a dream are running through our head while we are doing our early morning tasks. We wonder if we ever did get to that little village we were trying to find in the middle of the night—or maybe it takes us a few minutes to get over the fear we experienced while that big lion was trying to break down the door to the garage. We may think about this awhile on the way to work, but that generally is all there is to it. We may wonder a little bit why there was so much trouble in arranging the details for the air trip to Paris, but by the time we get to work the details gradually fade and the dream is lost—and along with it the opportunity to learn a little bit more about the nature of the reality we are making for ourselves day by day.

Record The Dream

The first rule in working with your own dreams is, of course, to record them. Otherwise, by the time you get to lunch, the dream, or most of its details, is lost and with it an opportunity. It takes a little time and effort to do this, but the rewards make it more than worthwhile. Remember, the more you do it, the easier it becomes to catch your dreams. Just like anything else, practice improves your performance.

The best time to catch the dream is during the period between when you wake up and when you get up. If at all possible, try to arrange your mornings so that you have five or ten undisturbed minutes after you have awakened and before you must get up. Just lie there and put your mind to recalling whatever you can from the night's dream activity. While you are doing this, be sure to be aware of the feelings or the emotions that the dream invokes in you. Let them run; think about them; and do whatever else seems necessary to understand them as

Interpreting Your Dreams

best you can. Once having done this, the next most important thing to do is to write the dream down. Keep writing materials at your bedside so that this is an easy thing for you to do. It is probably best to record your dreams in some sort of notebook—like a diary or a journal. This enables you to go back and review your dreams from six months or several years ago when you feel the need to do this. With a journal you can see how an ongoing problem in your life changes as the dream patterns about that problem change. Sometimes prophetic dreams are several months in advance, and it is really nice to have that dream on record when the event comes to pass. For instance, the first dream I had about the death of my father was a dream in which I saw him delivered of a baby. This symbolic content clearly indicated that the dream was talking about his coming death. The death occurred almost nine months after I had the dream which to me seemed appropriate and ironic all at the same time. All of these lessons for me would not have been apparent had I not been keeping my dreams in diary or journal fashion.

Some people use a tape recorder to keep a record of their dreams and this seems to work very well, particularly in the middle of the night when it is easier to pick up the tape recorder and tell the dream to it rather than having to turn the light on and write. Although this method is convenient, it is somehow not as effective as writing the dream down—and, of course, even after the dream has been taped it must be transcribed into your dream diary to give you an effective working record.

If nothing else is available to you, you can help keep the dream in your memory by telling it to somebody else. This gets a little awkward if the material in the dream is too personal. Also you have no guarantee that the other person is going to remember it any better than you do. I wouldn't recommend doing this with your bed partner in the middle of the night.

Those dreams that come up in the middle of the night are sometimes the most frustrating of dream experiences. Many is the time when I have awakened in the middle of the night because of a dream which at that time was very clear in my mind—even to the point where I was able to analyze it. I would say to myself, "Well, I'll certainly remember this," and would fall back to sleep only to awaken in the morning to the intense frustration of not being able to recall the dream or its interpretation. This experience is no different from that of many people. Because of this, I think it is very important to record these dreams on the spot rather than trusting your morning recall.

Work Out The Interpretation

Once you have your dream recorded, the next step is to work out its interpretation. In doing this, always keep in mind that one of the basic rules is that the purpose of the dream is to interpret the nature of the reality you are making for yourself. Your reality is a changing, fluctuating thing, hour by hour and day by day. At one time, things can be bright and cheerful and every adversity a challenge to be summarily dispatched. At another time, your energy seems low and you don't have that much interest in things happening around you and adversity seems almost overwhelming. All you want to do is withdraw into some good music or curl up with a good book. On other occasions, you are certain that your friends are working against you and that's why things went wrong—why you have to take measures to protect yourself in the future. A little while later you are so full of love and patience that you forgive perfect strangers for gross negligence or outright dishonesty. Some days you can do no wrong. On other days, you are obviously some bumbling idiot. Your dreams monitor all of this turmoil that goes on within you and try to keep it on an even keel. In doing so, they fluctuate in their emotions, symbols and outcome as much as you do, and on a day by day basis as well. In working with your dreams, keep in mind that, although they may change and fluctuate just as much as you do and sometimes over-dramatize things, rarely do the dreams let things slip by unnoticed the way you might.

As a matter of fact, those things that tend to slip by unnoticed during the day are often the very things that trigger off dreams. We tend to let things slip by because we don't want to deal with them. If we really looked at that twinge of anger we felt when our work was criticized by our good friend, Sam, we might have to change our reality by including the fact that from the time our brother started to tease us we have been much too defensive about listening to other people's viewpoints. And that night we may have a dream about being burned at the stake as a heretic to try to show us that we should listen to somebody else's viewpoint once in awhile instead of being so stubborn about our own.

Perhaps during the day, we were so impressed by a female co-worker's attractiveness and femininity that we really didn't notice that what she was up to in the work situation was not in our best interests. That night we dreamed we were having sex with the lady and she is on top doing all the work. The surface aspect of the dream is a follow-through on some of our sexual feelings in the situation which perhaps we need to understand a little better. The deeper implications of the dream are, of course, that this worker is giving us a real "screwing" in the negative sense of the term—which we also need to know about.

Free Association

Now that you have the dream recorded, what are you going to do with it? How can you extract from it these messages about yourself that may come from little half-noticed things the day before or may have to do with a momentous change in your life six weeks ahead. The simplest thing to do is to just think about the dream and see what it reminds you of. Freud refined this technique into what he called free association. All that means is that you put the dream in your mind and then just let your mind run with it without attempting to influence the direction it goes. It is still one of the best and easiest ways to work with a dream, but it does require a certain amount of objectivity. The process usually starts with recalling the events of the preceding day that the dream reminds you of, which in turn lead to other events further back in your life, until a pattern of one sort or another begins to emerge that will have meaning for you in your life today.

For instance, a patient of mine dreamed that she was stopped in her car at an intersection trying to turn right onto another street. In the dream so many cars were coming down the other street, she couldn't find an opening to make the turn and go on her way. When she started to associate to the dream, the first thing she remembered was that she had been able to buy her car after she began working. Then she recalled that she was trying to change her work situation by going in a new direction in the Institution where she worked. She then assumed correctly from the dream that she would not be able to find any job openings at that time.

The Intellectual Approach

Another way to work with a dream is the relatively simple intellectual process of listing in one column all of the major symbols in a dream. In the next column list the usual interpretation of the symbols. Then try to make a unified whole of this by fitting the interpretations together according to the way the symbols appear and interact in the dream itself. For example, a man had a dream in which he was journeying along a path that was winding up a mountainside. All along the path there were people hanging from ropes attached to trees and things. Some of these people had been there so long that they were dead. Others were still twitching. He was, of course, upset by this. Then a friend came along with a cart and helped him cut down these hanging people, both dead and alive. This dream has essentially three main symbols: the first being the path up the mountainside, the second being the many people hanging there, and the third being the friend and teacher who helped him cut them down. The path up the mountainside represents his journey toward achievement. The people hanging from ropes was initially a symbol that was difficult to understand— until he realized that in his journey towards achievement, he was a very busy individual with a bad tendency to let too many things and people hang, very often never getting back to them. His friend and teacher symbolized an aspect of his higher self. As a result, the individual was able to correctly interpret that the dream was telling him to correct his tendency of letting things hang until they were dead issues or forgotten and to clear these things up now, if possible, and not allow it to happen in the future.

This intellectual approach of breaking a dream into its components and working with each component's individual interpretation can be very useful in understanding a dream. Unfortunately, however, it very often results in a loss of the feeling tone of the dream. Oddly enough, even though it interprets the dream, it can be a way of evading some of the deeper issues that are included in each dream.

Focusing On The Action

Another way to work at the dream is to look at it from the standpoint of the action that takes place. For instance, a female patient of mine had a dream in which she was on the stage performing. As the performance went on, her mentor and teacher came up and handed her a silver ball. The inference she took from this dream was that she needed to work on her feelings concerning the idea that if she put on a good act, she could have a ball. Another example of this kind of interpretation was the short dream of a gentleman in which he found himself on a relatively high bank overlooking a beautiful lake. After some friends encouraged him, he jumped into the water and discovered to his pleasure that while under the water he was able to see a number of fascinating fishes. It had been at a time in his life when he was thinking about the possibility of learning the art of meditation. The dream encouraged him to take the plunge and enjoy the discoveries that he would find beneath the surface of his day to day existence.

Role Playing

When starting your work with a dream, it is always wise to first consider each symbol as being a representation of an aspect of yourself. If this doesn't seem to work after some effort, then, and only then, look at that symbol as relating to something other than yourself. Because the dream is about the reality you are making for yourself, most of its symbols will relate directly to you in one way or another. This is the reason for the following technique which consists of role playing various symbols in your dream. In this technique you become the person, animal or object in your dream as completely as you can and see what this brings to mind. This technique, at times, can be quite startling as to what it brings to the surface.

When starting on a dream, be yourself in the dream first. This means that as you think about the dream, you do your best to recreate in yourself the emotions and/or muscle tensions that you experienced while having that dream. Relive the dream experience. This reminds me of a dream that I had quite some time ago—actually before I got into the study of dreams. In this dream, I was in the back seat of a car being driven by my father who was accompanied by his sister in the front seat. They were asking me questions about how to get to the airport and I was telling them that I knew the way. As I did this, I became very frightened and the fear caused me to wake up. Because of the fact that my fear in the dream was so incongruous, immediately upon awakening I sat down and recreated that fear inside of myself and let it flow to where it would go. To my surprise, I ended up recalling incidents in my younger life that I had completely suppressed until that time. This little story is perhaps one of the best examples of why it is so important to run out whatever emotions you experience while in the dream as the first step in attempting to analyze the dream.

The same is true for the other sensations, muscle tensions and patterns that you experience while in a dream. For instance, I recall taking a nap on a Saturday afternoon many years ago. I awoke from the nap with the most peculiar crushing sensations in my head and shoulders and tension in my legs. I had no dream recall other than these sensations. I let them flow by lying there on the bed, perhaps not entirely awake. As they flowed, I suddenly found myself having the body image of an infant and I was being born. In the birth, I pretty much popped out after a number of peculiar, crushing, tingling sensations which I'm sure were my experiencing my mother's uterine contractions. After popping out, although I knew I was my adult self lying on the bed, I had a very clear-cut impression of the body image of an infant moving my arms and legs and crying. In addition to this, my visual sensations were most unusual. They resembled something like seeing things through ground glass—mostly large areas of color that moved one way or another. After this went on for a minute or so, I was suddenly lifted up with my feet slightly higher than my head. This startled me so much that I bounced out of the event and was entirely my adult self, lying on the bed, taking a Saturday afternoon nap.

This all occurred at a time in my life when I was motivated to relive my birth experience. The sensations I had were so definitive that there was no question in my mind that this was what happened at that time. Furthermore, it fits the family story concerning my birth. I was born at home. My father had almost a neurotic tendency not to call the obstetrician until he was sure that the delivery was underway. At the moment of my birth, the story goes that the obstetrician was washing his hands in preparation to attend my mother. While he was doing this, nature did its thing. As I was emerging, like Gargantua, I did give a mighty push with my legs. This, I feel, is another good example of how attending to the physical sensations and muscle patterns in a dream can result in surprising recalls and insights.

Another example of this same thing is the dream a patient of mine had in which he was wrestling with a mummy, something like one might experience in a horror movie. I had him relive the dream, first as himself in the struggle. He was successful in quickly tuning into the fear that he felt in the dream and the effort he felt in the struggle. The fear immediately reminded him of the anxieties he experienced when he was very young and found himself in a social situation either dressed or behaving in such a way that his Mommy (Mummy) would disapprove of. He immediately recalled an event in which he was attending a children's class and got himself excused to go to the bathroom. After coming back, he discovered he could not get his pants buttoned right, and experienced a great deal of anguish trying to figure out what to do. He recalled another event when he was with a group of children in a museum and had a slight but embarrassing accident and was teased about this by the children during the rest of the afternoon. There followed a long series of incidents in which his mother would be critical of his social behavior as a child. As he continued to re-enact the dream, he began to realize that in the dream he was winning the struggle with his Mommy. Following this I had him be the mummy in the dream, and he realized that he was actually something that had been long dead but which, for some reason, had come back to life to bother him again. He then noticed that it was no longer as strong as it had been previously. We then spent the rest of the hour working through many of the events that had surfaced because of this simple dream, with the result that he lost much of this fear.

From the stories I have told so far, I am sure you can see how really important it is to re-enact the dream inside of yourself, at least at those times when you are having difficulty in understanding the symbols. In fact, you should do this with most of the dreams that contain a very strong amount of feeling one way or another.

Perhaps it is a little bit more difficult to act out the inanimate objects in the dream, but usually it works just about as well. For instance, a client of mine had a dream in which he saw a monkey wrench in the works of a piano. The surface interpretation of the dream was quite obvious, hinging on the old phrase, "A monkey wrench in the works." However, when I had the client be the monkey wrench in the dream, he was able to realize that he had talents and strengths of specific nature and application. He very often tried to use these talents in the wrong type of situation—like trying to fix a piano with a monkey wrench.

In another instance, a woman dreamed that she was attending a party at her girlfriend's house. She was standing on the patio and was very frightened to see a fairly large snake lying in the grass nearby. When she re-enacted the snake in her dream, she realized that her attitude was such that she was turning into a real "snake in the grass" with respect to her girlfriend. This, in turn, surfaced a lot of material with respect to how she treated friends and acquaintances that she didn't like.

Keep On Trying

These are some of the various ways that you can use to approach your dreams when you are trying to understand them. If they don't work every time, don't get upset. You are going to dream again. And the next dream may give you a viewpoint and a series of symbols that are easier to understand—a result of the time spent working with the previous dream. I usually find it a lot easier to tell somebody else what their dream means than being able to work out the interpretations of my own dreams. It is not too often that you get the whole meaning of the dream in one sitting. But each time you work with a dream, you get a little bit here and a little bit there. Gradually those little bits add up to something significant, and every so often you have a whole dream that becomes obvious to you fairly quickly and easily.

Keep working at it. Every time you write a dream down, every time you think about it, every time you run out the emotion from it, you have done yourself some good. As time goes on, you get better at it and become more familiar with your own individual way of using symbols. Everybody has their own personalized way of using the symbols that appear in a dream and as you become familiar with this, it makes it easier to understand the dreams you are having. When it becomes too easy, your dream mechanism will probably start using the symbols in a slightly different way—just to keep the process interesting and intact.

As you get better at it, you begin to realize that your dreams contain all kinds of information. It can be useful in conducting your business. It can be helpful with your love life. It can give you a push in your spiritual development and even show you how to raise the kids. Once you begin to draw upon the wealth of material that is contained in your dreams, you start to grow as an individual and you are, in turn, better able to nourish yourself from the experiences you have day by day. As more and more special things occur in your dream life, you will begin to discover that more and more special things will also begin to occur in your waking life.

CHAPTER VIII

Prediction and Precognition

Dreams predict. They do this with such regularity that probably every major event in your life is first previewed by your dreams. Sometimes they will preview an event with such clarity and accuracy that it seems as though we have had a truly psychic experience and should maybe open up our own shop with a crystal ball. The proper term for this kind of an experience is to call it a precognitive one.

Predictive Dreams

Most of the time, however, our dreams are predicting in very much the same way as we make predictions for most of our behaviors. That is, we figure ahead from the data at hand. For instance, we rarely ever cross the street unless we are sure that we will make it safely to the other side. Or we put gas in the car because we predict that there is not enough in the tank to get us to work tomorrow morning. As a psychiatrist, sometimes I give a patient medicine to take because I have predicted that, without it, they may have a breakdown. From this you can see that most of our behaviors are based on what we feel will be the probable outcome depending upon the data at hand. This very often determines what we do in a given situation, depending upon what our goals or our purpose and intent for that particular situation happen to be. For instance, we get on the No. 73 bus because we predict it will take us where we want to go.

Sometimes we don't see enough of the situation. As a result, things don't necessarily go the way we hope they will. For instance, we may be very good at what we do at work and have an excellent production record. We are doing this because it will get us that raise we are hoping for. But perhaps at the same time we have overlooked the fact that we have a nasty, negative attitude towards most of our fellow employees that tends to be disruptive in the work situation. Until we correct that, our chances of getting the raise are not very good. We are not clearly seeing the nature of the reality we are making for ourselves.

Interpreting Your Dreams

A client of mine, in a situation like this, had a dream in which he was busy slashing at people with a sword. While he was doing this, he missed his train. After working with the dream he was able to see that his tendency to cut people down was keeping him from getting on the track that he wanted to be on. In another instance of a physical level dream, a client of mine dreamed that she went to the bathroom and discovered that the faucet was leaking. When she turned it on, it ran with blood. Two days later she began to show blood in her urine. In her dream, she had been trying to tell herself there was something wrong with her waterworks. Because of the dream she was able to deal with the situation with somewhat less distress than she might have without it.

Another client of mine, who was trying to save her marriage, dreamed that while she was doing the family wash her apron got caught in the washing machine and went down the drain. She felt that this dream was predictive of the eventual loss for her of the role of housewife. A few months later, despite her efforts at cleaning up the situation, her marriage dissolved—as she felt the dream was predicting. Another example that I frequently hear from women who are pregnant is a dream that accurately predicts the sex of their child—the simplest of these being when a dream focuses on something pink or something blue.

Very often a predictive dream is one that is trying to tell you that, if you maintain a particular attitude and set of behaviors, the probability of certain events occurring is very high. I am reminded here of the psychiatrist who had a woman patient whose attitude and behaviors made it highly likely that she would be raped. Indeed she had several dreams in which she was raped. Despite his admonitions, based both on his observation of her attitude and behaviors and her dream material, the woman persisted. A month or so later, she was actually raped.

I think you can see from the material presented thus far in this book that, in the process of doing their work of interpreting the nature of the reality we make for ourselves, dreams just naturally tend to present to us (either directly or by inference) the directions in which this reality will lead us. There is nothing extraordinary or supernatural about this process. We do the same thing all the time in our waking life. But in the dream state we are able to tune into those things that we are not as aware of while awake. Then when the dream comes true, we feel that we are psychic—which is not really so.

Incidentally, I think a very good rule to follow is that the purpose of prediction is to change the future. Fore-warned is fore-armed. By showing us the probable outcomes of things, our dreams can help us to either avoid them if they are bad (or at least soften the blow) or enhance them if the outcome is positive. Dreams don't just predict disasters. Very often they can be a pat on the back for a good decision or perhaps an encouragement to keep us going because things will probably turn out well.

Precognitive Dreams

On the other hand, dreams occasionally are capable of making predictions where there is no way that the information can be obtained by extrapolating ahead from the data at hand. Rather than calling this ability of dreams predictive, I prefer the term "precognitive." The simplest example of this type of thing is having a dream about a friend whom you haven't seen for years. Then the next day you get a phone call or a letter from this person or perhaps bump into them on the street. It is a very common experience and almost anyone can recall this happening to them at one time or another. This simple phenomenon seems to occur at a group level as well. Literature has a number of examples of disasters that were preceded by people dreaming about them from all over the country or, indeed, all over the world. The sinking of the Titanic is a good case in point.

These precognitive dreams can appear either in direct form—that is, the event is presented without any symbols or difficulty in interpretation—or they can be presented in symbolic form. An example of a symbolic presentation is a simple little dream I had about nine months before the death of my father. In the dream, I was standing on a ridge of earth that went crosswise across the street in front of the house where my parents lived and had lived for many years. I had a log and I was busy rolling the log down off the ridge (which was about four feet high) that I was standing on. I worked very hard on this dream but was unable to come up with any kind of interpretation for it. Only later did I realize that between the time I had the dream and the time of my father's death, my parents had sold the family homestead and moved into a building called the Highwood Apartments. At the time I had the dream, this particular apartment building was not even being considered as a place for them to move.

Most often precognitive dreams are more direct in the message they have to give, but you have to learn the knack of knowing the difference between a direct exposition of events to come and a regular dream. It is a very difficult thing to do. It is very much like telling the difference between having a cold and having hay fever. Sometimes they are mixed together.

I recall having a dream in which I was given the gift of a ring shaped in the form of a lion's head with a ruby in its mouth. When I mentioned the dream to my wife the next morning, she became excited and said she was planning to buy me such a ring in a few days for my birthday. But this lion had no ruby in its mouth.

This was a combination of a precognitive and a regular dream. The symbols of the ruby and the lion led into a great number of things that had settled out in my life at the time my wife was planning to give me the ring. The dream was a real compliment for a job well done at a symbolic level, as well as directly telling me what my wife was planning to do.

I know a woman who dreamed that her daughter and son-in-law were to be killed in an airplane crash. The dream occurred a few weeks before their wedding. They were planning to fly to their honeymoon destination. The woman did everything she could to prevent the couple from taking the flight but could not convince them. The flight crashed and the couple died. Turn about, on several occasions I have had people call me in the state of agitation to warn me of dire events that were to occur in my life. On one occasion I was supposed to be terribly depressed and about to commit suicide. On another occasion I was supposed to die in an airplane crash. Neither of these predictions were accurate nor fit into my life pattern at that particular time. In both instances the dreamers were making the mistake of not looking at the dream first as a comment on the nature of their own reality. When I appeared in those dreams, I was for the dreamers a symbol of some aspect of themselves.

It takes a lot of practice to spot those occasional instances of true precognition in your dreams. For most people it takes living through several of these experiences before they get truly good at spotting this kind of phenomenon in their own dreams. Even with precognitive dreams, the rule, "The purpose of prediction is to change the future," probably holds true.

Extrasensory Perception

I am not going to spend any time trying to convince the reader that E.S.P. is a natural phenomenon. This fact has been very firmly established. Research is now being directed at the mechanics of this phenomenon rather than the reality of it. The dream state, by its very nature, lends itself admirably to getting involved in extrasensory perception. As I have explained before, while we are asleep and dreaming, our belief systems, our convictions about ourselves and the world and the nature of the reality we are making have been put aside. Consequently, material that is not necessarily in agreement with this can be worked with. As a result, we can see things that we are not anticipating and become aware of things that don't fit our reality. At the same time, if we believe in these phenomena, it makes it easier to become aware of this aspect of our dreams after we wake up.

Although some scientists in the world are working very hard at trying to understand the mechanics of E.S.P. (that is, the biology, physiology, psychology and physics of these phenomena), they have not yet clearly defined what appear to be at least two levels of E.S.P. phenomena. Both of these are clearly illustrated in the sleep and the dreaming state. As best I can tell, these two phenomena have certain parallels with our senses of sight and hearing.

The long distance phenomena have been more than adequately documented by a series of experiments done by Stanley Kriptner, Ph.D., and Montique Ullman, M.D., in the early sixties at the Mimonides Hospital in New York City. In these experiments they selected pairs of people as experimental teams. They allowed one person to sleep with an electroencephalograph attached to his head. When the machine indicated that this person had entered into the dreaming state, a signal was sent to the second member of the team who was awake. That individual opened a sealed envelope containing a picture. He would stare at the picture and try to send impressions of it to the dreaming subject. As soon as the EEG machine indicated that the dreamer had stopped dreaming, he was awakened and immediately everything he had to say about the dream was recorded on tape.

No dreamer saw the picture as such, but very frequently the dreams of the subject would contain so many elements from the picture that an impartial panel of judges had to conclude that this was not coincidence. For instance, if the sending subject was looking at a painting of Central Park in New York City in the wintertime, the dreamer in his dream would see snow, would see a lake frozen over with ice skaters on it, would see a bridge going across the lake, etc. These experiments have been repeated a number of times since with similar results. Sometimes the distance separating the experimental subjects may be a few hundred feet and other times it may be several miles. Incidentally, some pairs of subjects in the experiment seemed to consistently achieve higher results than other pairs, but always the results of the group were significant and indicated that some kind of transference of information was going on while the sleeping person was dreaming.

Another example of the long distance E.S.P. phenomenon, which seems to relate somehow to the sense of sight, is the group dream phenomenon. For three years I met once a week with a group of people where, among other things, we shared and studied our own dreams. Towards the end of that time, it seemed that, because of our shared interest and empathy, we were at times able to get together somehow while we were sleeping. On one occasion, three members of the group dreamed of going to a particular house that was so unusual in its structure that there was no mistaking that all three had been to the same place in their dreams. On other occasions, members of that group would find themselves having a conversation with another member of the group. The next day they would call that individual to discover that the person they called remembered the same conversation—and, as a result, they were able to finish it or add to it during the phone call.

These and similar incidents seem to occur in any group that gets together to study their own dreams. It is my understanding that other dream groups have been able to deliberately program similar events among the members of the group while they are dreaming.

These phenomena in general seem to involve distances that are fairly great—a mile or more. Because of that, I feel that they somehow relate to our sense of sight which, as you know, is capable of going to the farthest star.

On the other hand, there is another type of E.S.P. experience that occurs in sleep—although not necessarily while we are dreaming. These experiences seem to occur only over distances that you can ordinarily hear or shout. Their mechanics appear to be related to the sense of hearing. In addition, this mechanism seems to operate as a warning or protective device in order to waken us or alert us to potential danger. The thing that tends to differentiate it from the long distance E.S.P. is that it does not necessarily occur while we are in the dreaming state but seems to occur at any time while we are asleep. It doesn't seem unreasonable to assume that in more primitive times, when man slept in less protected places, he needed this mechanism to warn him that perhaps a saber-toothed tiger or, worse yet, a man was lurking nearby. Because of the distance involved and other aspects of the phenomenon, it seems to relate more directly to our sense of hearing.

The most common example of this type of phenomenon is the way many individuals will awaken suddenly if someone else very quietly walks into the room and just stands there and stares at them. It is as though the sleeper has a sort of radar extending out a limited distance that warns him of potentially dangerous activity within that field.

Another more dramatic example of this kind of thing happened to a colleague of mine. His wife had gone to church and left their toddler son in a playpen in the living room. He was asleep and unaware of what she had done. Sometime after she left, he awakened with a start and without pausing to think immediately went to the living room. He got there just in time. It had been a cold winter morning and his wife had turned on an electric heater to make sure that the youngster was warm enough. The cord from the heater passed under an overstuffed chair. It was frayed and, just as he entered the living room, was in the process of catching the chair on fire. He had barely enough time to pick up the chair and throw it out the kitchen door. It burned so fast it was gone in minutes.

The last type of E.S.P. experience that occurs in dreams cannot be characterized as the clairvoyance or the sleep radar mentioned above. It is called astral traveling. In this phenomenon, sleeping individuals have the experience of leaving their bodies and traveling to a different location, perhaps miles away, in what might be called spirit form.

They usually recall rising out of their body and floating or flying to the other location. The reports of what they have seen can sometimes be confirmed by observers at the other location.

Some people seem to be able to train themselves to do this at will from an altered state of consciousness. There are many examples of this phenomenon reported in journals of parapsychology. Russian parapsychologists, whose interest is more often military application, have been intensively studying this ability.

The above are some examples of the various types of E.S.P. experiences that can and do occur in the dreaming and sleep state. As far as I am concerned, they are natural phenomenon that the sleep state lends itself to—and probably any or all of them can be enhanced and done deliberately by practice on the part of the individual experiencing them.

Lucid Dreaming

The last special case of dreaming that I wish to talk about is lucid dreaming. It has been enjoying increasing popularity for the past ten years or so. Lucid dreaming is being consciously aware of the fact that you are dreaming while you are doing it. Some people do it naturally and spontaneously and many others can be taught the technique. Once you become aware of the fact that you are dreaming while you are dreaming, your dreams change. They become more direct and, in turn, you can direct your activity in them. Psychic experiences begin to become more prominent and can also be directed. The eventual goal of the training is to be able to enter this dream-like state when you are awake.

The training usually begins by encouraging individuals to program themselves to become aware of dreaming while dreaming. This is done either by simple autosuggestion before falling asleep or by developing a more analytic attitude toward all experience, i.e. asking yourself every so often if you are dreaming or not. This attitude seems to carry over into sleep experiences and predisposes toward lucid dreaming.

This training and this awareness have great value and should be the subject of many books to come. The point is, however, that once you become consciously aware of the fact that you are dreaming, while you are dreaming, you can fundamentally change the nature of the dreaming process. These lucid dreams are no longer normal dreams and must be dealt with in a somewhat different way. As a result, I do not feel that they are properly the subject of this particular book. Working with lucid dreams and other E.S.P. dream experiences leads to a type of consciousness in which you are much more at one with your soul and spirit and more aware of what there is behind form and symbol.

Appendix

The following is a list of very common dream symbols. Almost all of them are mentioned in the text. With each symbol is a brief description of the way it may be used in your dream as well as the page number in the text.

This appendix has been included to give you a handy reference when working with your own dreams. Before using this reference, you should, of course, read the text. Any time a question about the symbol arises in your mind, it would be best to refer back to the text where the meaning of the symbol is in expanded form. Do not forget that everybody places their own individual twist on the symbols in their dreams and that the meanings given here may not really apply to you. We are merely giving the meanings that occur most often in people's dreams.

Adding machine—business, or how you are adding up your accounts in life. 38
Airplane—ideas, plans, flights of fantasy. 50, 55
Airplane crash—a bad outcome to what you are planning. 50, 90
Alligator—vicious speech, evil, destructive emotions rising from the depths of the unconscious. 61
Ancient history—your own early days. 50
Animals—usually refer to some aspect of the animal side of your nature. 59
Ankles—what you use to turn your feet to choose your path, the old way or the new; utilizing experience to correct mistakes of the past. 67
Another state—another state of mind. 49
Apron—signifies a matronly or housewife role. 88
Asleep—a situation where you are unaware. 53
Attorney—how you deal with your own forces of law and order. 56
Automobile—your body, but may symbolize the power of your mind. 54

Baby—a new responsibility, project, idea or attitude to which you may have given birth. 56
Backbone—the foundation of your being physically or mentally; also sometimes "spineless." 67
Backyard—things going on behind the scenes. 52
Bathroom—often refers to cleansing and/or getting rid of waste. 53
Battery—usually refers to nervous energy or storage of energy. 54
Battle—conflict within yourself. 51
Bear—your tendencies to be bearish, grumpy, overbearing; anger; tendency to crush or love too much. 60
Beaver—your tendencies to work very hard. 25
Bedroom—usually refers to sexual thoughts and feelings. 53
Bee—organized work that may be irritating yet probably productive; something may be bugging you; stings of life, unpleasant experiences, dangers. 62
Beetle—usually a minor irritation, annoyance. 62
Belt—a way of holding your public image together. 71
Bicycle—riding a bicycle usually symbolizes how you are maintaining your mental and/or emotional balance. 55
Bishop—an aspect of your higher self. 65
Bite—symbolizes aggressive behavior. 69
Black—the unknown, negative. 72
Blood—carries your energy. 69, 88
Blue—color of the spirit, truth, contemplation or completion; pale blue—struggle toward being "right on;" deep sapphire blue—being "right on;" murky blue—depression. 73
Bluebird—happy thoughts. 59
Boat—an endeavor with other people, probably spiritual in nature; voyage of life; managing to stay above water. 50
Bodice—the constricting feeling in your chest from sorrow and crying. 71
Body hair—sensitivity or coarseness. 69
Body sensations—refer to the area in which the sensation occurs; may be a recall of a past event. 69
Bowels—getting rid of waste or letting go. 67
Boy—a growing aspect of self. 25
Breast—has to do with nourishment, giving or receiving; self-awareness. 66

Brother—if seen clearly, attitudes from or concerning your brother; if seen indistinctly, attitudes toward mankind in general.   57

Brown—color of the earth and material things; riches; healthy; muddy brown—insecurity: situation that is "muddy."   74

Buffalo—pushing your way, trying to buffalo somebody or yourself.   60

Bug—minor irritations (what's bugging you?).   62

Building (Large)—an area of big concern in your life.   53

Bull—primitive or sexual energies; bull-headed, quick to anger.   59, 60

Bureau—symbolizes a place for stored things in our minds or life.   53

Bus—progress through life in areas of common consciousness with others, perhaps many stops on the way.   49, 54

Butterfly—the outcome of spiritual change.

Buzzard—tendency to scavenge; possibly a dietary warning.   59

Cadillac—vehicle equated with high station in life or money.   54

Calves—(along with ankles) signifies the utilizing of experiences to correct mistakes of the past to become more free; well-rounded personality.   67

Car—may symbolize the body or the power of your mind.   54

Cat—cattiness; negative emotions; independence of action.   61

Chair—that place in consciousness from which you direct things or rest.

Change of clothes—new occupation or job; a change of attitude.   71

Chased—fear of something within you catching up with you.   56

Chicken—chicken-hearted or afraid.   59

Child—a growing aspect of self; also young problems and responsibilities.   56

Choker—probably points to the neck and its meaning for you in terms of willfulness.   71

City—place in consciousness that you share in common; the place you are coming from.   49

Classroom—probably has to do with "school of life" and what you are or are not learning.   58

Cloak—symbolizes how you show your pride, either covered over or flamboyant.   71

Clothing—what we show of ourselves to the world; how we dress our attitudes; occupation; often refers to area of the body it covers.   71
Clowning—clowning aound.   55
Coat—how you identify yourself to the world, as well as protection. Change of coat may symbolize occupation.   27, 71
Cobra—the serpent fire within you; a kind of fundamental wisdom; our progress at physical, mental, spiritual integration.   61
Coloring hair—attempting to change the character of your thoughts or at least how you show them.   68
Colors—if strong and clear, a positive interpretation; if dark or murky, a negative interpretation; if pastel, a weaker interpretation. See individual colors for individual interpretations.   71
Costume—attitudes from its particular culture.   50
Crocodile—an avaricious, perhaps evil aspect that lurks in your mind.   61
Darkness—area of the dream that is poorly understood, "in the dark."   49
Dead people—usually indicate unresolved conflicts or attitudes having to do with or coming from the dead individual. If unidentified, may merely symbolize dead issues.   58, 82
Death—a change in your state of being, putting to rest a part of yourself, or a change in your relationship with the person who dies in your dream.   58, 80
Dirigible—awkward or grandiose flights of fancy.   50
Doctor—your own healing forces.   56
Dog—loyalty, faithfulness to a trust.   61
Domestic animal—a part of your animal nature that has been domesticated or tamed, i.e., integrated into your personality.   60
Dove—calming, peaceful type thoughts.   59
Drain—carries things away from your life or mind.   88
Drowning—overwhelming situation.   55
Dying—putting to rest an aspect of self, a change.   56, 58
Eagle—has to do with your heart and how your love or hate affects your behaviors.   59
Ears—relates to hearing, how well you listen.   68
Eating—has to do mostly with nourishment for the mind, the kinds of ideas you are feeding yourself or others.   55
Egg—contains unhatched potential.

Eight—strength, characterized by the coordination between spirit and matter; money; a strong number. 77
Elephant—strength, power, long memory; sometimes the ability to forgive and forget. 60
Eleven—physical mastery, sometimes weakness or conflict; at times a number of transitions. 77
Eyes—windows of the soul; sometimes the ego (I); inner or outer sight. 68
Falling—your support systems may not be working; anxiety, pride goes before a fall. 56
Family—attitudes and views that come from our family and how we are dealing with them. 57
Farm—an area in your life that is growing and producing. 51
Father—your attitude and views received from your father or perhaps toward him. 58
Faucet—may relate to your own "water works," bladder, kidneys, etc. 88
Feet—a real understanding of the purpose of all the other parts of the ego and a belief in this; the purpose of your being. 68
Fighting—a conflict within yourself. 55
Fingers—interpretation depends primarily on what activity they are engaged in. 69
Fire—anger; may represent a cleansing process. 52
Fireman—that aspect of self that puts out the fire of anger. 57
Fish—generally has to do with those forces that nurture your spirit, spiritual food. 25, 62, 83
Fishing—searching for spiritual food and knowledge. 25
Five—the number of change; occasionally stability in that it is the middle number of the nine digits (the only thing permanent is change). 76
Flowers—beautiful thoughts. 53
Foreign country—a foreign state of mind. 49
Forest—an area of unexplored or untapped growth; may symbolize body hair. 49
Four—the physical, material, organized aspects of life (four-square); the material expression of your thought processes. 76
Fox—wily, foxy, cunning aspects of self. 59
Friends—those aspects of yourself that come from or relate to these friends. 57
Frog—ancient symbol for evil; uncleanliness; the idea of change is also expressed here (that is, a tadpole into a frog). 61

Front yard—those more public or "on-show" aspects of your life. 52
Games—playing games with self or others. 55
Garden—an area in your life where you are working towards a harvest of some sort.
Genitals—may depend upon their activity in the dream, excretory or sexual. 67
Giants—an exaggerated aspect of yourself. 50
Giraffe—head high, far-seeing; long distance between head and heart; distortion of self; stiff-necked. 60
Glove—how we clothe or protect our thoughts. 71
Goat—stubborn; perhaps tendency to butt in.
Gods and goddesses—symbolize higher aspects of self. 65
Gold—spiritual richness, divine intelligence; the color has to do with a stabilizing, healing aspect; the metal itself may symbolize your inner worth. 74
Green—a healing and growing color.
    Blue-green —more healthful and trustworthy.
    Yellow-green—may be deceitful and perhaps indicative of poor health. 73
Guiding figure—an aspect of higher self. 65
Gun—may be phallic in significance; also symbolizes a way of imposing your will on someone. 53
Hair—what comes out of your head—thoughts. 68
Hair dressing—how we dress our thoughts. 68
Hallway—the way you let people inside yourself. 52
Hands—expression of thoughts. 66
Hanging—to let something hang, "hang it up." 82
Hats—very often how we dress our ego. 71
Hawk—symbolizes very high aspects of spiritual development, (see Egyptian symbology). 59, 60
Head—ego, mastery of conscious will, coordination of spirit and mind. 66
Heart—has to do with love and hate and your drives towards one or the other. 67
Hidden room—unused potential within yourself. 53
Hill—the top may symbolize an aspiration you are climbing toward or a vantage point within your psyche. 51
History—your early days. 50
Home—the place where you live inside of yourself. 52
Horse—the power of your emotions, physical or animal energies; sometimes a message or messenger. Is the horse tame or wild? 60
Hotel—a temporary situation. 53

Ice—frozen assets.

Intercourse—may be a direct expression of a sexual wish; most often symbolizes intercourse at other different levels.   81

Jewel—a polished truth

Judge—how you judge your relationships to natural laws.   56

Kitchen—area of yourself where you are "cooking something up."   53

Knees—the beginnings of learning to use the fruits of experience through flexibility.   67

Knife—the ability to cut people up, either verbally or mentally.

Lake—an area of tranquility in your life where spiritual resources may be multiplying.   83

Lavender—the color of after-completion, seeking, moving ahead to a new challenge.   74

Lemon juice—may symbolize a need for more acid or sour in your system.   25

Levitation—ideas or excitement without foundation; sexual excitement.   55

Lice—minor irritations or perhaps a way of indicating you or someone else is lousy.   62

Light—an area of good awareness (a lot of light on the subject). Turning on the light indicates our attempts to illuminate the subject.   49

Lightning—a sudden perhaps traumatic illumination, things are changed dramatically and drastically by a "bolt out of the blue."   51

Lights—source of internal illumination   49

Lion—your pride, or tendency to be regal.   35, 59

Lost—an area in your life where you no longer know how to get where you are going.   56

Mailman—delivers the message.   57

Man—if a general symbol, probably has to do with how you relate to mankind in general.   59

Man next door—someone who is positioned close to where you live within yourself.   37

Mice—things nibbling away at your resources; curiosity or minor irritations.   61

Midget—a stunted aspect of yourself.   56

Money—relates to your sense of worth, not only at an economic level, but particularly at a mental, social and ego level.   74

Monkey—playfulness.   60

Monkey wrench—one of your inner tools.   85

Motel—temporary situation. 53
Mountain—a very high aspiration (the abode of the gods). 51
Mouth—more often has to do with what comes out of your mouth rather than what goes into it. 68
Mud—social difficulties or disapproval. 51
Mule—tendency to be stubborn. 59
Mummy—some old attitudes that are being preserved but not used. 85
Murder—an attempt to finish off an aspect of yourself. 28
Naked—socially exposed, but very often exposed and unprotected in other ways as well. 71
Neck—has to do with your willfulness, be it with or against nature and God. 66
Necklace—relates to neck. 71
Necktie—relates to neck; may symbolize organs in the chest. 71
Neighbor—someone close to where you live within yourself. 37
New person—new ideas and attitudes that may be entering your life. 57
Night—a time when things are not as well illuminated, known, or understood as during the day. 49
Nine—completion of the cycle; balancing of the body, mind and spirit. 77
Nose—ability to discriminate; may be social, such as "looking down your nose at someone." 68
Numbers—see text numerology. 75
Old books—your own ancient history. 50
Old sea captain—aspect of higher self. 65
One—the beginning, the "I am;" unity, ego. 76
Opposite sex—your complementary self; your ability to effectively be dominant or receptive (see text). 65
Orange—friendship, thoughtfulness and consideration of others; fruits of the earth. 73
Owl—wise, can see through the darkness of ignorance; keeps its own counsel. 59
Patio—that area of consciousness where you socialize with family or friends. 85
Peacock—excessive pride, self-love. 59
Physicist—attitudes towards physical sciences. 37
Pig—pigheaded, gluttony, slovenly. 59, 60
Piranha—avaricious aspects of the subconscious. 62
Playboy—attitudes towards this life-style. 37

Pointing—pointing the finger, getting your attention.   55, 66
Policeman—your internal aspects of natural law and order; factors that make you feel guilty or intimidated.   56
Porch—the mental platform within yourself from which you look at the world.   52
Prostitute—lower aspects of self; perhaps a tendency to sell or prostitute yourself.   57
Purple—the energy to maintain what we have achieved; "purple passion" when carried to extremes.   73
Rabbit—a lot of sexual activity, timidity.   25, 61
Radio—how you are "getting the message."   53
Rain—depressing emotions; may be cleansing, renewing.   51
Rainbow—promise of better things to come; a new beginning, hope.   51
Rat—carrier of disease; people gossiping about you, or in other ways making you uneasy.   61
Red—energy, anger, ego, sex.   72
Refrigerator—area of storage within yourself.   53
Reins (loins)—how we deal with our fellow man; friendships; being outgoing and loving or inhibited by self-centeredness.   67
Relative—attitudes and ideals from this association.   50
Right turn—usually a turn in the good or right direction.   82
Ring—symbolizes a promise or achievement.   89
Robin—thoughts preceding a new beginning.   59
Running—what are you running toward or away from? How are you running?   55
School—usually has to do with the "school of life."   58
School books—what you are learning or supposed to learn in the "school of life."   58
Sea—the origins of life and spirit; its depths show much about our subconscious.   25
Sea captain—aspect of higher self.   65
Seven—the number of spiritual awareness that can lead to attainment, hence good luck.   77
Sex—our ways of interacting and obtaining gratification with other people.   81
Shark—avaricious tendencies in the subconscious.   62
Shot—a sudden devastating impact from another; may be sexual in nature.   53
Shoulders—how we think and show off our thoughts.   66
Silver—reflection of light from God; the color has to

do with stimulation at a mental level; the metal has to do with our inner sense of wealth and worth, perhaps a quick mind. 74
Silverware—relates to how we feed ourselves mentally. 53
Sister—attitudes and views about or towards this individual. 28, 56
Six—the balance and integration of physical and mental, body and mind working together; well-rounded, indicating beauty and strength and a high sense of order. 76
Smell—our ability to discriminate; bad smell may indicate something is rotten. 75
Smoke—indicative of the fire of anger or smoldering resentments. 52
Snake—signifies either temptation or wisdom. 59, 61, 85
Snow—frozen assets, a time in life when things are immobilized. 52
Socks—how we dress or protect our understanding. 71
Son—an immature part of self, often material in nature; growing that may involve problems or responsibility. 25
Song—try to get its meaning from the title or words. 75
Spider—a designing individual who weaves webs that get us all tangled up. 27, 59, 62
Spine—foundation of our being physically, mentally, morally or spiritually. 67
State—another state of mind. 49
Stethoscope—may symbolize occupation; may symbolize how you are listening to your heart. 38
Stomach—has to do with nourishment, taking in or giving out. 67
Store—a place to make decisions in acquiring things. 53
Stored items—ideas, talents, aspects of self that are in storage. 53
Storm—usually relates to emotions, emotional storm. 51
Struggle uphill—our progress towards our aspirations. 55
Swamp—an area of our life or consciousness that slows us or mires us down. 51
Swimming—how we make our progress in areas of higher consciousness. 55, 83
Table—that common restricted level of consciousness where we deal with other people. 53
Tableware—aspects of ourselves useful in dealing with

other people or taking in food for thought. 53
Tame animal—an aspect of our animal nature that is integrated. 60
Taste—the type of taste may indicate a need for this substance physically, such as bitter, sour, sweet, salt. 75
Tax collector—aspect of self that indicates payment is due. 57
Taxi—ideas and powers that we use temporarily in our way through life. 54
Teacher—aspect of self concerned with learning what we need to in the "school of life." 65
Teeth—the gate of the tongue; very often has to do with how we control our speech; may be involved in aggressive biting behavior. 68
Telephone—communications; how we are getting through to others. 53, 57
Telephone man—assists in communications. 57
Teller bank—keeps our individual accounts. 57
Ten—a new beginning at another level; a return to unity. 77
Thigh—our outgoing or ongoing nature, either physically or socially, based on the fact that we are beginning to see or understand things better. 67
Thirteen—a symbolic death and rebirth, a beginning afresh, change from which we cannot come back. 77
Thirty-three—symbolizes spiritual mastery. 77
Three—the number of mental creations, associated with ideals and concepts. 76
Ticket seller—sets the price we pay to enter the arena. 57
Tied up—forces that keep us immobilized. 55
Tiger—the emperor of beasts; a powerful symbol for physical integration; also stealth, stalking. 59, 60
Tires—how we mentally contact the world to withstand the everyday wear and tear; if flat, perhaps we have lost our bouyancy at a physical or mental level. 54
Toes—may have to do with our ability to maintain our balance and push ourselves forward. 69
Tooth—if lost, may indicate a lost friendship. 68
Touch—what do we touch and how? Have we lost touch? 69
Train—going with a group of people of like mind; "on the track." 49, 54
Trees—fruit trees symbolize bounty that we are growing and harvesting; otherwise, a solid growth in our life. 50

Truck—an aspect of our work; a heavy load we may be carrying. 54
Turtle—long-lived, slow; strength, longevity and patience. 61
T.V.—the process of obtaining our internal picture. 53
Twenty-two—the number of physical mastery. 77
Two—the first division of the whole; two aspects are needed to create—strength when working together, weakness in division. 76
Under water—below the level of the conscious. 83
Undressed—socially exposed, or in other ways unprotected. 71
Unidentified person—how we relate to our fellow man or woman. 57
Uniform—symbolizes our trade or occupation. 71
Valentine—a report on the condition of our heart, actually or figuratively. 26
Vermin—minor irritations. 62
Violet—the color of after-completion or seeking. 74
Vulture—tendencies to scavenge and locate likely prospects. 59
Wash—how we are cleaning our selves, our thoughts, our spirits. 88
Water—cleansing, revitalizing, contaminating; its interpretation depends very much on its context in the dream—see text. 52, 83
Wedding—a union or partnership being formed. 56
Whale—a tremendous aspect in your subconscious. 62
White—purity, innocence, cleanliness. 72
Wind—usually has to do with the emotions and mental turmoil such as a whirlwind. 51
Wild animal—animalistic parts of self as yet not integrated or tamed. 60
Wires—nerves or connections in your psyche. 54
Wise man—aspect of higher self. 65
Wise teacher—aspect of higher self. 65
Work area—that part of your personality in which you do your work. 53
World—usually symbolizes your own personal world or sphere of influence.
Zero—usually placed in a number for emphasis. 77